Hamlyn

London · New York · Sydney · Toronto

Gardening is Fun

with
Percy Thrower

illustrated by Marilyn Day

photography by Philip James

Contents

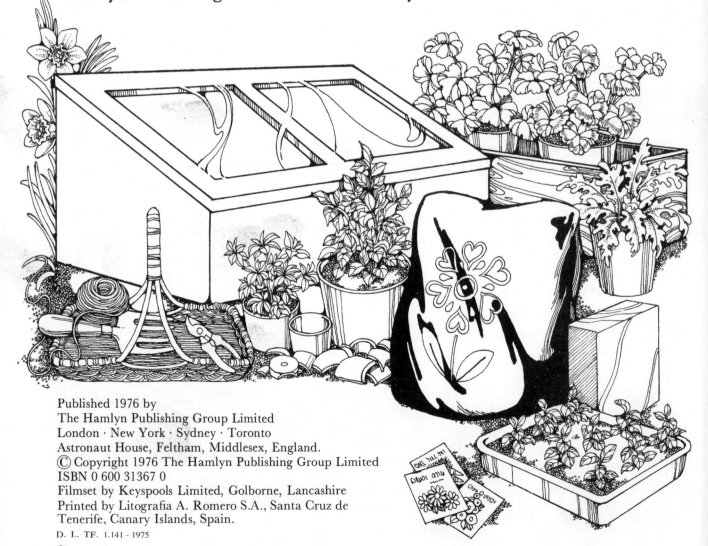

Published 1976 by
The Hamlyn Publishing Group Limited
London · New York · Sydney · Toronto
Astronaut House, Feltham, Middlesex, England.
© Copyright 1976 The Hamlyn Publishing Group Limited
ISBN 0 600 31367 0
Filmset by Keyspools Limited, Golborne, Lancashire
Printed by Litografia A. Romero S.A., Santa Cruz de
Tenerife, Canary Islands, Spain.
D. L. TF. 1.141 - 1975

Introduction

I'm in a fortunate position, for gardening is not only my living, it's my hobby as well. I started off when I was at school with a small plot of land where I grew some lettuces, radishes and a few annual plants for cut flowers. Then, my father gave me a plot in the garden at home. This was not as good as the one at school; it was under a walnut tree and I had to contend not only with the shade cast by the tree, but also with the walnut roots which made the soil difficult to cultivate and took out of it much of the goodness which my plants would need. As a result, the lettuces were not very hearty; the radishes were not too good and the annuals rather spindly. From this I learned that the majority of plants need a piece of sunny ground which is neither overshadowed by trees nor full of their roots.

I soon discovered that you must be patient and that when you sow a seed you can't expect it to be up the next day; you have to allow a week, ten days or a fortnight according to the weather. Everything is dependent on the weather, and on the soil too. The ideal soil is a nice medium loam, but the average garden does not have this, so start off by learning what you can do to the soil to improve it. Then begin by growing a few easily cultivated plants, like hardy annuals, and perhaps a few vegetables, and gradually move on to the more difficult subjects such as rock and water plants.

I was always told that you don't go out into the garden in your Sunday suit. You put on an old pair of shoes, or better still, wellingtons, especially if the ground is on the moist side, an old pair of trousers or jeans, and a thick sweater or anorak until you warm up. If you will be handling plants which are prickly you will need a pair of thick gloves to stop your hands from becoming pincushions. If your anorak is not waterproof, wear a raincoat – you can get very wet running from the bottom of the garden to the house in a sudden downpour.

The purpose of this book is to interest you in things that grow and things that surround you; the trees, the hedges, the wild flowers and the plants in the garden. The more curious you become, the more you learn, the more you will want to learn; the joy of gardening, I find, is that you have never finished learning.

Tools
you will need

To start off with you will need four basic tools: a spade, a fork, a rake and a hoe. If you have these four you can do most of the important garden operations. If you find that the normal sized spade and fork are too large, you might find that a border fork and spade are better – these are slightly smaller than the normal types and are easier to manipulate. As you become more ambitious you will need a trowel, a hand fork, a pair of secateurs, for cutting small branches off trees and shrubs, and probably a pair of shears for hedge clipping.

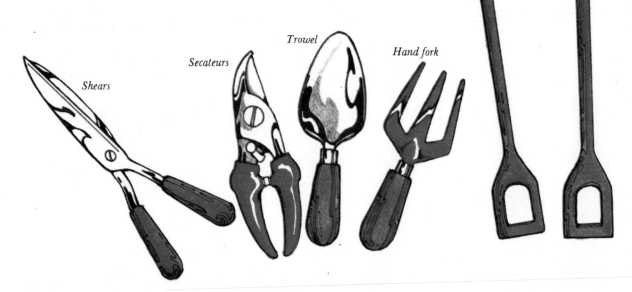

Spade   Fork

Shears   Secateurs   Trowel   Hand fork

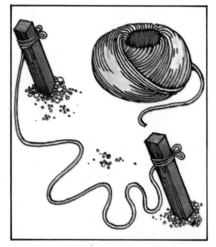

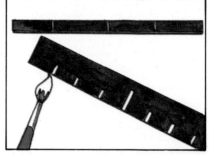

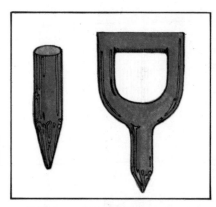

Many small tools you can make yourself. A garden line, essential for marking out a straight line, can be easily made from two short lengths of 3 cm. square wood and some strong twine.

A measuring rod can be made from a narrow length of wood by painting it black and then marking off each half metre in white paint. On the first half metre mark off twenty 2·5 cm. spaces and place a short mark at every 10 cm. interval. You can use your measuring rod along with your line for planting vegetable seedlings at the correct spacing.

Dibbers for pricking out seedlings can be made from 8 cm. lengths of 1·25 cm. dowelling, or even from the old teeth of a wooden rake. A broken spade or fork handle becomes a tool; simply sharpen the end and you have a dibber for planting cabbage or cauliflower seedlings in the open.

If you intend to buy a spade or a fork, buy a good one. This will cost you a little more than one which is cheaply made, but it will probably last you a lifetime. If you can persuade someone to buy one for a birthday or Christmas present, so much the better, but make sure that you go and choose it yourself, so that you get one which you find comfortable to work with and easy to use.

When buying a spade, the first thing to do is to feel the weight of it. Is it going to be too heavy? Hold the spade in your hand, just above the blade – it should balance on your hand like a pair of scales; this will show you that the spade is well constructed and, therefore, easier to use. Stainless steel spades and forks are good, but are usually very expensive; a good tempered steel one will be quite adequate.

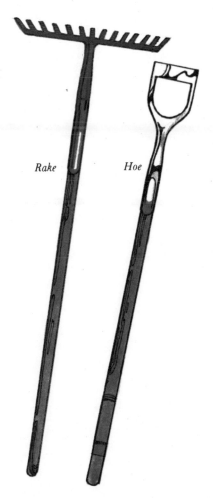

Rake   Hoe

It is very important that you take good care of your tools. Tools which have been cleared of soil and mud and wiped with an oily rag after each gardening session will be much easier to use the next time and they will also last much longer. Take as much pride in your tools as you do in your garden, and clean them and hang them up in the shed or garage after they have been used.

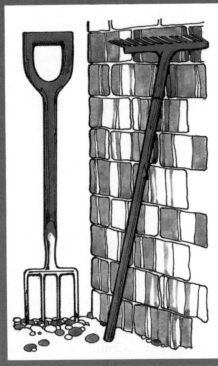

Safety hints

Working with large tools with sharp blades and prongs can be very dangerous if you do not take care. Wear stout shoes or boots when you are digging and keep the spade and fork blades away from your feet. Never leave a fork lying on the ground with the prongs sticking up – it is easy to walk into it and spear your foot. Never leave a rake lying on the ground – if you tread on the head you will almost certainly get a smack in the face and probably a black eye as well! Always stand a rake against a wall with the head uppermost.

Many gardening tools are sharp and many garden plants have thorns so if you do cut or prick yourself, always wash the cut carefully and apply a dressing to keep the dirt out.

Most garden accidents are caused as a result of carelessness; if you store your tools correctly and respect chemicals and sharp implements it is unlikely that you will come to any harm.

9

Where shall I have my plot?

Thinking of the conditions your plants are most likely to appreciate, look for a spot in the garden which is not overshadowed by trees, not next to a hedge where the roots will rob the soil of its nutrients and not on a piece of land which is exposed to wind. In other words, choose a site which is sheltered but open to sun and air, and you have the ideal spot.

Start off with a small plot. You can always extend it if you need more land, provided that space is available, and it is much easier to cultivate a small piece of land and keep crops well looked after and weeds controlled. It is amazing what you can grow in only a few square feet of soil.

Never be frightened to mix flowers and vegetables; it is not essential that you keep them both on distinct pieces of ground as long as all the crops have plenty of light, air and soil.

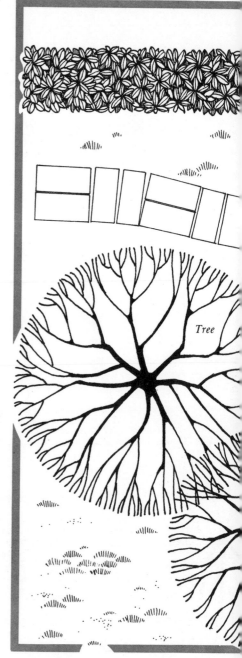

Tree

Before you decide what to grow on your plot you will have to find out something about the soil. There are three important things you will need to know about; firstly, drainage of the soil.

It is very important that apart from holding water for plants to take up and use, the soil should also be able to get rid of any excess water so that the plants are not drowned and can also take in air through their roots. Take a look at the soil on your plot on a rainy day. If it looks muddy and pools of water are standing on the surface of the soil for some time after the rain has passed, the chances are that the soil is badly drained. Go out and pick up some pieces of the soil while they are moist. Rub a sample smoothly between your finger and thumb; if you get a shiny surface which looks polished you probably have a soil with a high percentage of clay in it. Clay particles are very small and cling together so tightly that drainage is made difficult. If the soil feels gritty to the touch, it probably contains a lot of sand or silt, and will not stick together in the way that clay does.

Soil broken down and stirred into water will separate into humus, clay and sand.

All soil is made of broken-down rock – sand and clay being just that. It also contains something called humus. Humus is very important; it is the broken-down remains of plants and animals and it supplies the living plants with essential nourishment as well as keeping the soil rich and healthy. What sort of soil is in your plot?

Carry out a simple test by drying a sample of soil from your plot, breaking it down with your fingers and then stirring it into a glass of water. Watch what happens. The particles which float on top will be humus, the ones which sink to the bottom fastest will be sand, and the ones which settle out more slowly and make the water cloudy will be clay particles. By observing which particles are in abundance and which are absent you will get some idea of the composition of your soil.

If your soil is badly drained and also has a lot of clay in it, adding well-rotted manure or peat will improve the drainage. If your soil is lacking in either humus or clay, manure or peat will also help to improve the water holding capacity and the fertility.

Hedge

Path

Plot in sunny position

Tree

Rhododendron

Carnation

The rhododendron prefers an acid soil; the carnation can do well in limy soil.

Collect leaves in a simple wire cage. Rotted down they will enrich the soil.

The second important consideration about your soil is the amount of nutrients it contains. Plants use a wide variety of these which are their way of feeding. The three main plant nutrients are nitrogen, phosphorus and potassium; these can be made available to the plants by applying a general fertilizer which contains these sources of food for your plants, and also by ensuring that there is plenty of humus in the soil. Applying leaf-mould (rotted-down leaves) and well-rotted manure will ensure the presence of humus in your soil.

Thirdly, it is important that you know how much lime is present in the soil. Some plants, such as hydrangeas and carnations, tolerate lime, others, such as rhododendrons and heathers, do not. If a soil contains a lot of lime it is said to be alkaline, if it contains a little it is said to be acid.

Plants which do not like an alkaline soil will go yellow if the soil contains too much lime; this is because the lime stops them getting at another important nutrient – iron. Most plants will grow well in a soil which is only slightly acid and contains sufficient nutrients for them to survive.

You can test your soil to see how much lime it contains by placing a teaspoonful of the soil in a saucer, mixing it with some rainwater and placing on it a strip of litmus paper which you can buy from a chemist. If the paper is blue and turns bright red when it meets the soil, the soil is very acid and will need an application of lime. If the paper turns pinkish, the soil will be slightly acid and all right for most crops. If the paper goes a deeper blue, the soil is alkaline and an application of an acid peat will be helpful.

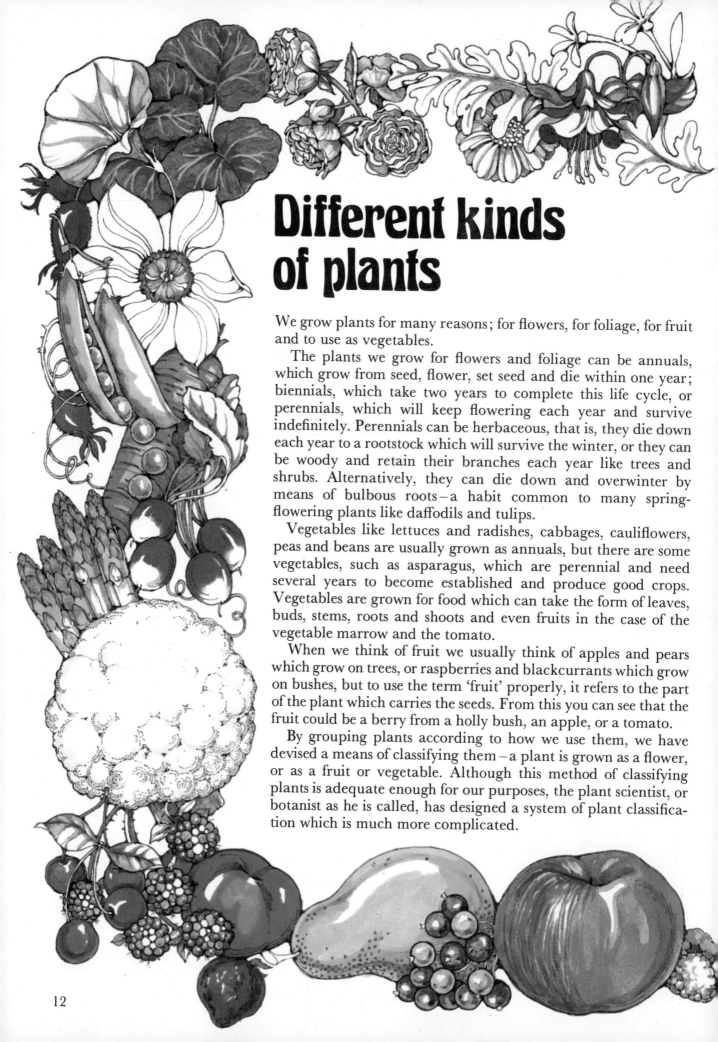

Different kinds of plants

We grow plants for many reasons; for flowers, for foliage, for fruit and to use as vegetables.

The plants we grow for flowers and foliage can be annuals, which grow from seed, flower, set seed and die within one year; biennials, which take two years to complete this life cycle, or perennials, which will keep flowering each year and survive indefinitely. Perennials can be herbaceous, that is, they die down each year to a rootstock which will survive the winter, or they can be woody and retain their branches each year like trees and shrubs. Alternatively, they can die down and overwinter by means of bulbous roots – a habit common to many spring-flowering plants like daffodils and tulips.

Vegetables like lettuces and radishes, cabbages, cauliflowers, peas and beans are usually grown as annuals, but there are some vegetables, such as asparagus, which are perennial and need several years to become established and produce good crops. Vegetables are grown for food which can take the form of leaves, buds, stems, roots and shoots and even fruits in the case of the vegetable marrow and the tomato.

When we think of fruit we usually think of apples and pears which grow on trees, or raspberries and blackcurrants which grow on bushes, but to use the term 'fruit' properly, it refers to the part of the plant which carries the seeds. From this you can see that the fruit could be a berry from a holly bush, an apple, or a tomato.

By grouping plants according to how we use them, we have devised a means of classifying them – a plant is grown as a flower, or as a fruit or vegetable. Although this method of classifying plants is adequate enough for our purposes, the plant scientist, or botanist as he is called, has designed a system of plant classification which is much more complicated.

Dandelion

Bugle

Groundsel

Great Sundew

Mint

Scots Pine

Plant names

Everything on earth has a name and plants are no exception to the rule. We can, without too much difficulty, tell the difference between a daisy and a dandelion – one has a yellow flower and the other a white one with a yellow centre. The leaves are quite different too – the dandelion has longer leaves than a daisy and the edges of the leaves are jagged. However, if we look at the flowers together, we will see that they are of a similar shape and layout; they are both composed of many small florets. The daisy and the dandelion are, in fact, in the same plant family. The botanist, like ourselves, has grouped plants according to their similarity – not according to what they are used for, but according to their resemblance to one another. This grouping helps the botanist to see how plants have developed over the years.

Having grouped the plants into families, the botanist must give them names. It is easy to call a plant a daisy or a dandelion, but you cannot tell from these names that they are related. Another problem arises if we consider foreign languages. A Chinese or a Russian gardener would not understand what a dandelion was – he would have a completely different name for it. To avoid these problems, a universal system of plant nomenclature, or naming, was adopted so that the plant was given an official Latin name, which is used throughout the world. This system of naming was devised by an eighteenth-century botanist called Carl Linnaeus.

The plants are grouped, according to their similarity, into families – and then into smaller groups called genera and species. So, if we look at the Latin name of the daisy, *Bellis perennis*, we will see that it is composed of two parts. The first name is the generic name – the plant is in the genus *Bellis*. The second name is the descriptive part, known as the specific epithet – a complicated title for the half of the name which tells us something about the plant. The two names put together show the plant species. *Bellis* tells us that this plant is related to other plants called *Bellis* and the name *perennis* tells us that the plant is perennial. The second part of the name is always informative. Here are a few examples:

Dandelion:	*Taraxacum officinale*	*officinale:* can be used as a herb
Groundsel:	*Senecio vulgaris*	*vulgaris:* common
Bugle:	*Ajuga reptans*	*reptans:* creeping and rooting
Great Sundew:	*Drosera anglica*	*anglica:* from England
Mint:	*Mentha rotundifolia*	*rotundifolia:* round-leaved
Scots Pine:	*Pinus sylvestris*	*sylvestris:* wild, not cultivated

On other plants the descriptive names will tell you the colour of the flowers, whether the plant is large or small or if it is scented.

The Latin names of plants are very interesting but not always easy to remember; for the average gardener it is easier and quite sufficient to use the common English name which the plant was given by our ancestors – unless, of course, you go to China and wish to ask for a daisy!

13

The plant and its parts

To get the best flowers, fruits and vegetables from our plants it is important that we grow them well. The plant consists of four main parts, each of which has a different function:
The roots; the stem; the leaves; the flowers.
An understanding of the functions of these will help us to provide the plant with the conditions it needs.

The roots form the part of the plant which is normally under ground. They usually occupy as big an area in the soil as the branches and leaves occupy above the ground and they consist of many fine, hair-like roots as well as the larger ones which we can see when we dig up a plant. The roots are usually long and thin but they can be fat and swollen, as in the case of turnips and radishes, or long and pointed in the case of carrots. The thin roots are called fibrous roots, and the fat or pointed ones, tap roots. When you are weeding in the garden you will find that the weeds which have tap roots, like the dandelion and dock, are very difficult to pull up. This is because the roots are fulfilling one of their main purposes – that of anchoring the plant firmly to the ground.

Apart from holding the plant firm, the most important function of the roots is to take up water and dissolved nutrients which the plant will use to manufacture food. If the roots are deprived of water, the plant will wilt; if the roots are deprived of nutrients and the plant is grown in poor soil, the plant will become weak, spindly and stunted and will bear poor flowers. Always make sure that the soil is well nourished and that plants are well watered in dry weather. The roots also need air, so the soil must not be waterlogged. Do not give a plant too much water.

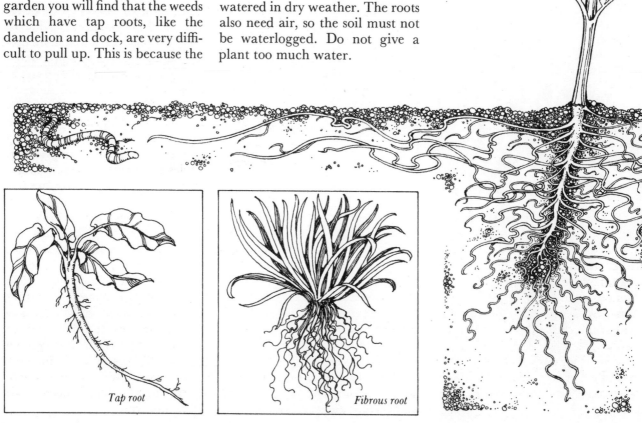

Tap root

Fibrous root

The fruit of the apple swells out beneath the flower, which dies away as the apple grows.

The flowers of the plant have only one purpose: to produce seeds and ensure the survival of the species. To do this they have to be pollinated; they may be brightly coloured to attract bees, butterflies and other insects, or they may be highly scented for the same reason. Dull-coloured flowers will probably be wind-pollinated; that is, they will produce much more pollen than the insect-pollinated plants and it will be carried on the wind to other plants of the same species. If a plant is successfully pollinated and fertilized, seeds will be produced. When growing plants like marrows, raspberries, apples or any other fruits, we have to ensure that the flowers are fertilized, or we will not get any fruit.

When growing plants for flowers only – such as hardy annuals – we do not want fruits to be formed; they will not be particularly decorative and the plant will spend energy on producing seeds rather than more flowers. For this reason it is always best to take the dead blooms off plants which are grown for their flowers. If this is done the plant may flower again and not spend time manufacturing seeds we do not want.

The leaves are the plant's factories. Here, the nutrients and water transported by the stem from the roots are used in the manufacture of sugars which the plant uses as food. To manufacture these sugars the plant needs light and carbon dioxide – both can be easily provided if the plant is placed in a sunny and airy position. For this reason you should be careful where you dig your plot.

The stem is really the skeleton and veins of the plant. As the skeleton it holds the plant upright, displaying the leaves and flowers to advantage, and, as the veins, it transports the water and dissolved nutrients from the roots to the leaves and flowers. It can also transport nutrients down the stem for storage in the roots. The fat roots of turnips and radishes act as stores for food which is not used instantly by the rest of the plant.

Sowing seeds

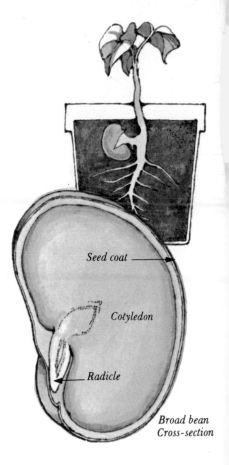

In a small, dry, wrinkled seed are all the characteristics of the parent plants, preserved until you want to use them. If you look at a large seed like a pea or bean, you will be able to see what a seed consists of.

On the outside of any seed is a coat which protects the seed from being damaged. If you look to one side of the coat you will see a 'V' shaped piece of tissue which lies close to the side of the seed. This is the first root, which is known as the radicle. Just above it, but hardly visible, will be the first shoot, and the largest part of the seed, which the root and shoot are attached to, consists of two large seed leaves known as cotyledons. Some plants have only one cotyledon. The seed can be perfectly preserved in this state for a long time – provided it is kept cool and dry. Some seeds will last for many years, others – like some vegetables – for only one season.

To see what happens when a seed germinates – when it starts to grow – a useful experiment is to grow some mustard and cress. You can observe what happens in the early stages, and then you can eat the experiment!

Carefully follow the instructions below and you will soon have a thriving crop.

Seed coat

Cotyledon

Radicle

Broad bean Cross-section

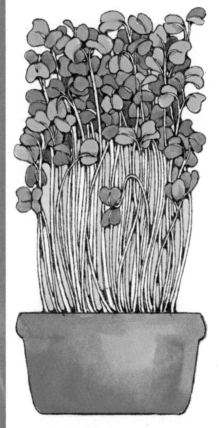

Mustard and Cress

The mustard and cress can be bought in separate packets and you can sow it on either a clean flannel, or some blotting paper.

Take a shallow tray – a small baking tin is ideal – place in it a piece of flannel, or whatever you choose to use as water-holding material, and pour sufficient water into the bottom to soak it.

Now for the seeds: the two kinds are best sown separately and mixed when they are cut, so you will need two trays. The mustard will grow more quickly than the cress so it should be sown three days later. Sow the seeds thickly and evenly over the flannel.

Cover the seeds with a sheet of paper to keep out the light and make sure that the flannel does not dry out. Lift the paper each day and see what is happening.

The seeds will get fatter and fatter and eventually they will send out their first root – the radicle.

This will be followed by the shoot and at this stage the paper should be removed. Stand the seedlings on a window ledge where there is plenty of light, but make sure they are sheltered from strong sunshine which may scorch them.

When the mustard and cress seedlings are about 2·5 cm. to 4 cm. high, cut them off the flannel with a pair of scissors, mix the two together and eat them!

If you clean the roots off the flannel after you have cut the crop, you will be able to sow again. Sow some seeds at three to five-day intervals and you will be able to have a succession of mustard and cress to use in salads and sandwiches.

1. The flannel is placed in the tray and soaked.

3. Cover the tray with paper; keep the flannel wet.

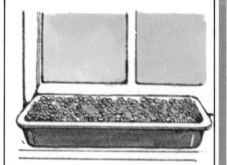

5. Stand tray on windowsill, but out of strong sunshine.

2. Sow the seed, the mustard three days after the cress.

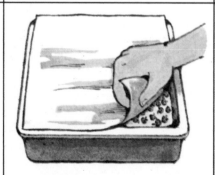

4. Lift paper each day: when shoots appear uncover tray.

6. The seedlings are ready to be eaten when 2.5-4 cm. high.

A display of bulbs

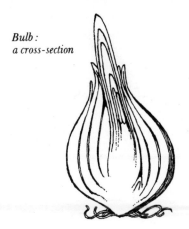

Bulb:
a cross-section

We usually think of a bulb as being a root, but it is really a cluster of small, fat, scaly leaves which stays beneath the soil. If you cut a hyacinth or daffodil bulb in half you will see the leaves packed tightly together and in the centre of them will be a very small flower bud. The small, flat piece of tissue at the base of the bulb is the plant's stem and attached to this are the roots, as can be seen in the illustration on the right.

Although bulbs are not quite so well protected against damage as seeds are, they can also be stored, but for a more limited period of time. They can be bought in shops in their dry state – that is, without the leaves which they send out above ground – and planted where they are to flower. The bulb is a food storage organ which works a year in advance. If you buy some bulbs in a shop and plant them in your garden, the flowers and leaves they carry will have been formed by the bulbs the previous year; if they were well grown then, the flowers and foliage will be of good quality. The flowers the bulbs carry the year after you plant them will have been formed in your own garden, so the test of whether you are growing them well will be at that stage.

The most common and widely grown bulbs are those which flower in spring: daffodils, tulips, hyacinths, snowdrops and grape hyacinths. The crocus is also common – but the crocus is not a bulb, it is a corm. Whereas the bulb is a cluster of leaves, the corm is a short, fat, condensed stem, so although it may at first glance look like a bulb and serves the same purpose as a food storage unit, it is in fact solid flesh covered with dry leaves. Both bulbs and corms are grown in the same way. The cyclamen is another popular plant which grows from a corm. The popular corms and bulbs are easy to grow and make a fine display.

Daffodil   *Tulip*   *Snowdrop*   *Crocus*

Flowers for Christmas

One of the interesting operations in the gardener's year is the forcing of bulbs for Christmas and New Year flowering. The word 'forcing' is used to show that we are forcing the bulbs to flower before their normal flowering season. The most popular bulbs for forcing for Christmas are the hyacinth and the narcissus. (Narcissus is the Latin name for the daffodil and is applied to all the various kinds.) By bringing the bulbs into flower early, we can provide a welcome splash of colour in the home when little else is in flower in the garden, and a cheerful Christmas display.

18

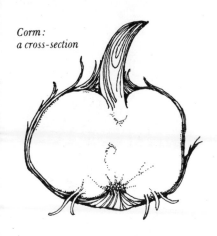

Corm: a cross-section

To force bulbs for Christmas flowering, plant them in late September. First of all, decide how many pots you want to force and of what colour and kind of bulb. Narcissi come in a range of colours and forms – some with orange trumpets and others with cream, yellow and white ones. There are also completely white kinds and even double forms.

A few varieties which I find very attractive are: Golden Harvest (yellow), Fortune (yellow), Actaea (white petals and a small orange and yellow trumpet) and Cheerfulness (double cream).

Of the hyacinths, Jan Bos (dark red), King of the Blues, Pink Pearl and L'Innocence (white), are highly decorative and sweetly scented. For a bowl about 20 cm. in diameter you will need three hyacinths. Always plant bulbs of the same colour in a pot – if you mix the colours the bulbs will probably flower at different times and the effect of a bowl full of colour will be lost. Narcissi are best planted in pots where they can be placed in layers, allowing more room for their roots.

Plastic containers are the easiest to use but you can also grow bulbs in hollowed-out logs, pottery containers, and tiny ones can be planted in plastic yoghourt containers, as illustrated overleaf. Pots can be bought at most garden shops or general stores and should have plenty of drainage holes in the base. Choose one about 20 cm. wide and 10 cm. deep for the hyacinths and use the deeper 20 cm. plant pots for the narcissi.

1. The bulb fibre is well soaked in a bucket of water.

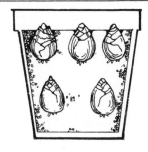

2. Narcissus bulbs: one layer is planted under another.

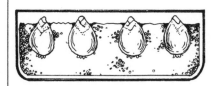

3. Hyacinth bulbs: one layer in a shallow pot.

4. The bulbs are placed in a cool, dark cupboard.

5. At about 2.5 cm. put the narcissi in a shady place.

6. Hyacinths can be taken out when the flower buds show.

Bulb fibre is the most convenient substance in which to plant them. It can be bought in various sized bags and it consists mainly of peat, with a little charcoal and leaf-mould added.

Before planting the bulbs, give the fibre a thorough soaking in a bucket of water. Bulbs need a lot of water and will not grow successfully if the fibre is dry. For the hyacinths, fill the pot to within 8 cm. of the rim and sit the bulbs on the fibre. Now fill in round them, with the fibre leaving the 'nose' of the bulb sticking out; firm the fibre well. For the narcissi, place 5–8 cm. of fibre in the bottom of the pot and put four bulbs on to

this, sitting them firmly in the fibre. Add another 5 cm. of fibre and then place a second layer of about six bulbs into the pot. Cover this layer, like the hyacinths, leaving just their noses showing; by planting two layers in this way you will get more flowers to a pot. Both kinds of bulb should then be placed in a cool, dark cupboard. Look at the bulbs frequently and when the narcissi have grown about 2·5 cm. high they can be taken out of the cupboard and placed in a position which is shady – not on a windowsill in bright sunlight.

The hyacinths can wait a little longer – when you can see the top of the flower bud, which will be

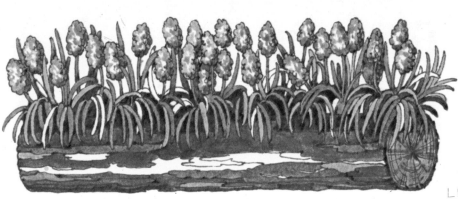

green at this stage, they can be taken out of the cupboard and given the same treatment.

The period when the bulbs are in the cupboard will last from four to six weeks. Watch the plants carefully now for water; never allow them to dry out completely. After about a week they can be put in a sunny spot.

As the narcissi begin to grow they will need staking to stop them falling over. Thin green canes are the best; these are quite cheap and are easily obtainable. Place three or four around the edge of the pot and tie two pieces of fine green twine around them – one about 8 cm. from the base and the other about 5 cm. from the top; the canes should be about 30 cm. tall. Small twiggy branches can be used, in fact they look more natural than canes if they are used carefully. Hyacinths do not always need supports and unless they look like falling over, let them stand as they are. The same green canes, broken in half, can be used for them if they look like toppling.

After they have flowered, the bulbs can be planted in the garden where they will flower next year. Plant them to the level of the soil in the pot and allow them to die down. Don't remove the foliage until it is brown and dead. The food manufactured in the leaves will be taken down to the bulb and if the leaves are removed too early the bulb will be starved. It is a good idea to mark the area where you have planted your bulbs so that you do not forget where you have put them; it is very easy to dig them up by mistake.

Not all bulbs will stand forcing like narcissi and hyacinths. Crocuses particularly come to mind. These are best planted straight into the garden where they can grow and flower naturally. Plant bulbs in the garden with a trowel, planting them with as much soil on top of them as they are deep; that is, a snowdrop bulb which is 2 cm. deep should be planted with that amount of soil on top of it, an 8 cm. deep Narcissus bulb should be planted 8 cm. deep.

The best time to plant bulbs in the garden is late September. Some kinds worth trying are: snowdrops; grape hyacinths; tulip; daffodils; scillas (squills and bluebells).

Grow an annual border

One of the most colourful features in any garden, I always feel, is a planting of annuals. Although, unlike other plants, they have to be grown from seed each year, the effort put into raising them is amply repaid by a colourful display.

If you grow only hardy annuals, they can be sown straight into the soil where they are to flower. Half-hardy annuals are usually sown in a greenhouse or garden frame and planted out later on, when the weather is more favourable.

For ease of cultivation, I will explain how to construct a border consisting entirely of hardy annuals.

Hardy annuals are not particularly demanding plants; they will put up with a fairly dry soil which is not necessarily rich in nutrients. But, like all plants, they will grow better in a fertile soil and will appreciate extra water in very dry weather. The spot where you intend to grow your annuals should be open and sunny, a shady spot will produce only weak and spindly plants. The area need not be very large, say 1 m. × 3 m., or smaller if your space is limited; you could even grow the annuals around a patch you intend to use as a vegetable plot. Begin by digging or forking the ground over to a depth of about 20 cm. in December or January – don't go on the soil when it's too wet – but digging it at this time of year will make sure that the soil is well aired and broken down by the wind, frost and rain.

January is the month to decide which annuals you want to grow. Annuals I have found attractive are cornflower, larkspur, clarkia, godetia, nasturtium, sweet pea, annual chrysanthemum, calendula, virginian and night-scented stock and sunflower. You can buy the seeds in packets from a garden shop or you can order them from a seed merchant.

If you order them, do so in good time, for January is the busiest period of the year for the seedsman and your order may be delayed. When you are deciding what to grow, make a rough sketch plan of your border and draw in the patches of different plants. This will give you some idea of what to grow in the different parts of the border, and will show which plants will be next to which.

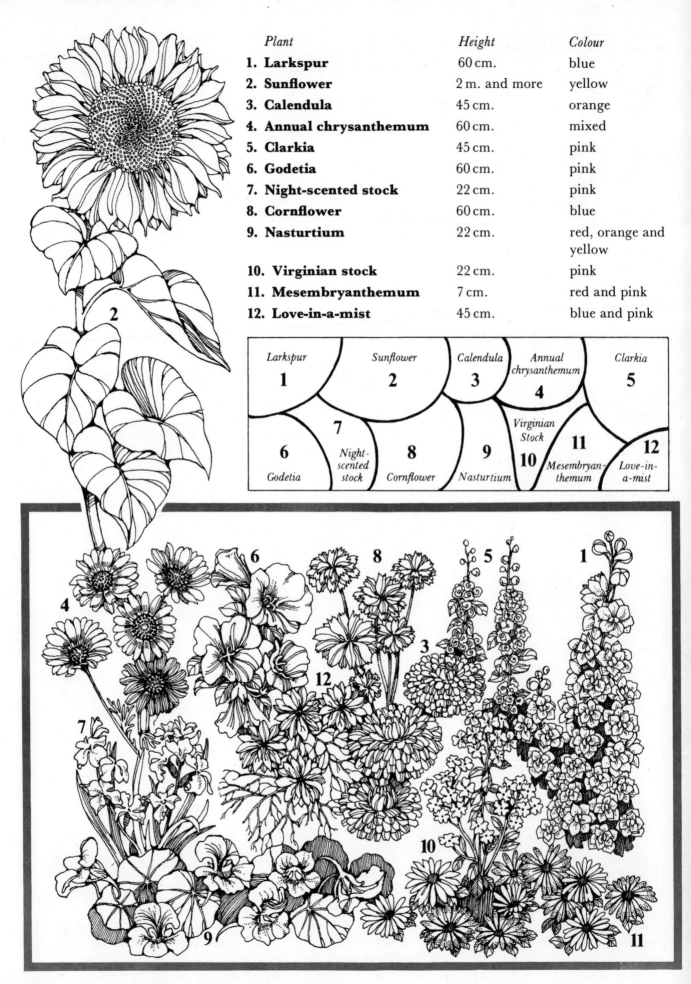

Plant	Height	Colour
1. **Larkspur**	60 cm.	blue
2. **Sunflower**	2 m. and more	yellow
3. **Calendula**	45 cm.	orange
4. **Annual chrysanthemum**	60 cm.	mixed
5. **Clarkia**	45 cm.	pink
6. **Godetia**	60 cm.	pink
7. **Night-scented stock**	22 cm.	pink
8. **Cornflower**	60 cm.	blue
9. **Nasturtium**	22 cm.	red, orange and yellow
10. **Virginian stock**	22 cm.	pink
11. **Mesembryanthemum**	7 cm.	red and pink
12. **Love-in-a-mist**	45 cm.	blue and pink

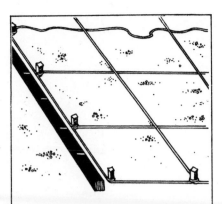

1. Mark your plot into square metres with rod and line.

2. Sprinkle general fertilizer at 55 gm. per square metre.

3. Break down the soil and rake it level.

4. Trace out your plan: place seed packets on each area.

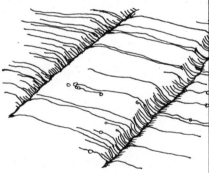

5. Furrows for sowing are made at correct depth.

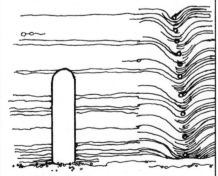

6. Seeds are sown, furrows raked over and labelled.

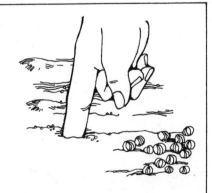

7. Larger seeds can be pushed in with your finger.

In late March or early April, sprinkle some general fertilizer over the soil at the rate of 55 gm. to the square metre. Mark out the squares on the soil using a measuring rod and line, weigh the fertilizer, and apply the correct amount to each square.

In mid-April, when the soil is moist, go out on the plot and break down the soil with the back of a fork or with a rake. Work the soil down until it is fairly fine and then finally rake it level. This gives a good surface on which to mark out the areas to be occupied by different plants according to your plan. To do this, the rake handle or any pointed stick is drawn across the soil and shapes for the plants are marked out like a jigsaw puzzle. Generally, the larger the plant is, the larger the area it will need. An idea of the sort of design you can make is shown in the drawing opposite. This is only a rough plan. Vary it as you wish, remembering the size of the plant in question.

Bringing some of the taller plants to the front helps to give the border better contours and avoids the appearance of a large slope from back to front.

When you have marked out the shapes of the areas to be occupied by the different plants, place the packets of seeds on the shape they will occupy. Now write out a label for each one – plastic labels are best, they are not very expensive and if you use a waterproof felt tip pen on them they will remain legible for several months.

Start at the back of the border and sow a patch at a time. A general rule to remember when sowing seeds is that you always sow a seed one and a half times its own depth. This is a rough guide: don't go as far as getting out a ruler to measure the depth.

To sow the seeds, run a small length of stick over the surface of the soil and create shallow furrows of the correct depth for the seed. Do this over the whole of the patch and then open the packet and sow the seed thinly along the furrows or drills as they are called.

Then take the rake and gently pull the soil at right angles to the drills, filling them in. Press the label into the soil and the job is finished. Do this in each of the shapes, the ones at the front of the border being the last to be completed. Large seeds like nasturtiums can be pushed in at wider spacings with your finger, as in the illustration below.

The seeds will take anything from a week to a fortnight to germinate depending on the weather – the colder the temperature the slower the process.

When the seedlings are about 2·5 cm. high, pick a day when the soil is moist, and go out and thin them. The smaller ones need to be thinned to a spacing of about 22 cm. and the larger ones to 30 or 45 cm. By picking a showery day I find that the roots come out of the soil more easily. The plants removed can be used to fill gaps left by those seedlings which have not germinated.

The seedling stage is probably the most critical as regards watering. Do not let them get too dry or they will keel over and probably never recover.

The smaller plants like stocks and nasturtiums will need very little further attention, other than a watering in very dry weather, but the larger plants will need staking to stop them falling over. Twiggy branches provide the most natural looking support if they are used thinly. They can be collected in winter from old shrub prunings and inserted into the soil when the plants are about 15 cm. tall.

Remove the flowers as they fade and the plants will bloom more freely. Cut the stems for indoor decoration whenever you need them. But be sure to leave enough for a good colourful display in the garden.

Thin out seedlings at about 2.5 cm. high.

Taller plants need support: a twiggy branch is ideal.

To add variety to the border, sweet peas can be grown up tripods at intervals. Tripods are easily made from three stout canes each about 1.25 m long. Push them into the soil to form a triangle and tie the tops together with wire or strong twine. Three seeds can be sown at the foot of each cane and as they grow they can be trained up the canes. They will eventually start to cling with their tendrils and from then on will need no further encouragement giving a bright sweetly-scented display.

Sweet peas grow well up a
tripod of sticks.

Some annuals have flowers
which are everlasting, that is, they
can be cut and dried. Some you
may like to try are acroclinium,
statice and helichrysum. The
flowers should be cut when they
are beginning to open and hung
upside down in a dry place. When
completely dried out they can be
used as you would normal flowers
for indoor decoration, the only difference being that they do not need
any water. They are particularly
welcome in winter when there is a
shortage of flowers in the garden.

Dried flowers—a colourful
winter flower arrangement.

Grow your own vegetables

Vegetables are very rewarding plants to grow; besides having the enjoyment of cultivating them, you also have the pleasure of eating them. When you have tasted your own vegetables, brought straight from the garden to the kitchen and table, you will probably agree that your efforts have been well paid. They are always far more delicious than the tinned or frozen varieties.

By growing only a small selection of vegetables on a small piece of land you will be able to eat fresh crops for most the year and also save a good deal of money. As with annual flowers, what you grow is governed by the amount of space available but if you are able to use a plot which is about 2·50 m. × 2 m. you will be able to grow a fair range of crops.

The vegetables I suggest you try are radishes, lettuces, carrots, peas, broad beans, beetroot and spring onions. The plan shows where you could position these crops on the plot.

1. Dig over the plot in autumn.

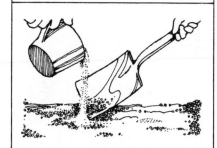

2. In March apply a general fertilizer.

2·40 m.

7 cm. 30 cm. 60 cm. 90 cm. 1·15 m. 1·35 m. 1·65 m. 1·95 m. 2·15 m.

2 m.

Radishes / Broad beans / Carrots / Peas / Lettuces / Peas / Lettuces / Beetroots / Spring onions / Herbs

The better the vegetables grow, the better the crop we get and so it is very important that the ground is well prepared and fertilized so that the plants form strong and healthy growth. As for annuals, the ground should be dug over in the autumn. I always like to dig as deeply as possible for vegetables, so that the roots can penetrate the soil well. In late March, usually about ten days before the first seeds are sown, apply a general fertilizer to the soil at a rate of about 55 gm. to the square metre. A general fertilizer is one which contains balanced proportions of the most important plant foods, nitrogen, phosphorus and potassium, symbolized on the bag by the letters N, P, and K.

The main sowing period for vegetables is late March and April. Seeds are easily obtained from a seed merchant or shop but in some years certain seeds may be in short supply and substitutes may have to be made. Always buy good quality seed which has a well-known brand name. For the crops

3. Rake the soil to a fine texture before sowing.

5. Use a cane to scrape out a drill to the right depth.

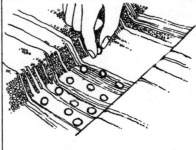

7. Peas: three rows in a drill 20 cm. wide and 5 cm. deep.

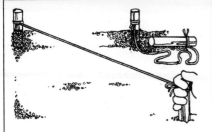

4. Keep your rows straight by using a garden line.

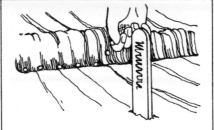

6. Sow the seeds and fill in: label each row.

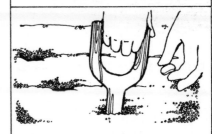

8. Broad beans: sow with dibber, 10-15 cm. apart.

9. Broad beans: pinch out the tops to discourage blackfly.

I have mentioned, the table (p.28) shows how and when to sow, and how far apart to space the seeds. Break the soil down to a fine texture with the rake before sowing. The seeds should always be sown in straight rows. To do this, use the garden line. Peg it in at one end, take the other end of the line and walk across the plot, tightening it before you stick the other end into the ground. Stand on the line at one end and walk backwards over it, scraping out the soil with a cane to the required depth.

After sowing the seed, gently fill in the drill with the rake, raking the soil inwards and taking care not to dislodge the seeds. Always sow on a day when the soil is just moist and label each row clearly after sowing.

Hoe regularly between the rows of plants, taking care not to push the hoe too deep and damage the plants' roots. Water all crops in very dry weather and remove any plants which have finished cropping or have died. Do not be frightened to sow quick maturing crops in vacant areas.

Keep the plot clear of weeds with regular hoeing.

Radishes: *Sow 1·25 cm. deep from March onwards.*

Radishes grow very quickly and they should be eaten as soon as possible when they are large enough. Sow only a third of the 2 m. row at a time and sow each third at two-week intervals. The second third should be sown two weeks after the first third and so on. Sow the seeds thinly so that they fall about 10 cm. apart. When the first crop has been eaten, sow some more seed in its place. Keep on doing this for as long as you require them. Keep radishes well watered when the ground is dry and avoid leaving them too long or they will become woody. Harvest from April to September.
Varieties: French Breakfast, Cherry Belle.

Broad beans: *Sow 5 cm. deep from late March onwards.*

Sow the seeds individually along the row using a dibber and space them between 10 and 15 cm. apart. When the beans have produced two or three flower clusters, pinch out the tops of the plants; this discourages attacks by blackfly which frequently appear on broad beans. Pick the pods as soon as they are about 15 cm. long and quite swollen. Pick frequently to encourage the other pods to mature. Harvest the beans from June to October.
Varieties: Aquadulce, The Sutton.

Carrots: *Sow 6 mm. deep from April to July.*

The soil for carrots must be extra well cultivated or the roots will become forked and distorted. Sow the seed very thinly in the drill so that you do not have to thin out the seedlings later on. If they are thinned, they may be attacked by a fly whose grubs eat the roots and spoil the crop. To see whether the carrots are ready or not, pull a sample up every week or so from the end of May. They should be ready for harvesting in June and will carry on maturing for several weeks.
Varieties: James Scarlet Intermediate, Chantenay Red Cored.

Peas: *Sow 5 cm. deep from March to June.*

Peas are best sown in a flat-bottomed drill. Take out a 5 cm. deep drill with the rake, making it 20 cm. wide. Sow the seeds with your fingers and space them about 5 cm. apart making three rows of seed in each drill. Rake over the soil and firm it. Water the young plants in dry weather. Most of the new dwarf varieties can manage without any kind of support, but if you find that they are straggling over the plot, they can be held up by twiggy branches inserted as frequently along the row as necessary. Harvesting can begin about three months after sowing and can continue for several weeks. Pick the pods from the bottom of the plants first, removing them when they are fat and full.
Varieties: Little Marvel, Kelvedon Wonder.

Radishes

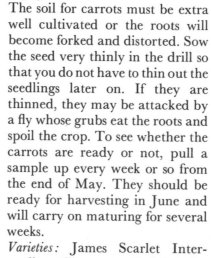

Peas

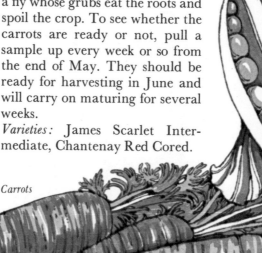

Carrots

Broad beans

Lettuce: *Sow 1·25 cm. deep from March onwards until August.*

Lettuce are very useful vegetables to grow as an intercrop; that is, between two crops which are slower growing but which will eventually need the space occupied by the lettuce. You will see that on the plan I have placed one row between two rows of peas and another between the peas and the beetroot. When these crops mature there will probably be no room between them. Sow the seed thinly. When it germinates and is about 5 cm. high, thin the plants out, leaving one every 23 cm.

The thinnings can be planted at the side of the plot and used to fill gaps if any seedlings die off or are eaten by slugs. Pick the lettuces as soon as they are large enough to give a good supply of leaf. The thinnings can be used to replace plants which have been picked and in this way they can prolong the season. Like radishes, several sowings can be made, as long as there is sufficient room. Water the plants well in dry weather.

Varieties: There are two main types of lettuce: the cabbage lettuce, which forms a heart rather like a cabbage, and the cos lettuce which has longer leaves which are crisp and juicy.

Cabbage lettuce: All the Year Round, Webb's Wonderful.

Cos lettuce: Lobjoit's Green, Little Gem.

Beetroot: *Sow 2·5 cm. deep from April to July.*

The round-rooted types of beetroot are best for early sowings and should be sown in groups of three at a spacing of about 15 cm. in the row. Thin the seedlings when they emerge, leaving one at each point. Like radishes, they can go woody and because of this it is useful to make small sowings at intervals (a third of a row, as in radishes) and eat them as soon as possible.

The first sowings can be harvested in July and if some seed is sown every two or three weeks in the early stages, the season will be quite long. Make sure they have plenty of water in the growing stages. The skin of the beetroot is very tender so take care that you do not bruise the roots when you lift them. Ease them out of the soil by pulling at the base of the leaves and twist the foliage off with your hand before taking them in for cooking.

Varieties: Crimson Globe, Sutton's Globe.

Spring onions: *Sow 1·25 cm. deep from March onwards.*

Spring onions are another fast-maturing crop. They can be sown quite thickly in the drill, in a part of the plot which has been particularly well cultivated; they like a very fine soil, as do the carrots. Water them well in the early stages, and as the stem bases begin to swell at ground level, thin some out for eating. Pick in this fashion all the time, taking the fattest onions first. Like the radishes, lettuces and beetroot, you can make successive sowings.

Varieties: White Lisbon is the best and most widely grown.

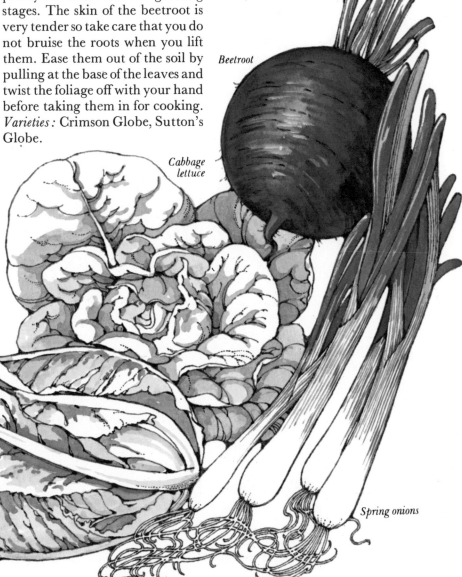

Beetroot

Cabbage lettuce

Spring onions

Cos lettuce

Herbs

As well as growing plants to eat, we can also grow plants to use as flavouring for meat, fish and even vegetable dishes. Apart from being useful in this way, the plants often have a pleasing appearance and scent, and lend themselves to being planted in a less formal way than vegetables. Plants grown for use in this way are known as herbs.

Parsley: *Used in sauces and as a garnish for potatoes and fish dishes.*
Sow the parsley from March to August 6 mm. deep in a patch which you can design to fit in between other plants. Thin the seedlings out to one every 15 cm. and remove any flower stems. Remove the leaves on a rota basis, so that no one plant is weakened. Although the parsley will persist for several years, it is more succulent if it is sown each year.

Mint: *Used to make many sauces, particularly for lamb, and to make jelly and drinks.*
Mint is one of the easiest herbs to grow, but it spreads by means of underground stems and can take more land than you have to spare. The best way of containing it is to sink an old, bottomless bucket or bowl into the ground, so that the rim is at ground level; plant a piece of mint in this and allow it to spread within the bowl. The plant will grow very rapidly and the tips should be used as they are the most tender part of the plant. You can plant mint at any time of the year.

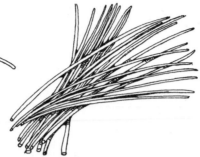

Chives: *Used in salads, sauces, soups and egg dishes.*
Chives are a kind of onion and their leaves have a mild onion flavour. Sow the chives 1·25 cm. deep in March in a patch and thin the seedlings out, to leave one every 15 cm. Water them well when young. The plants will grow into tufts and the leaves can be cut off in small quantities with a pair of scissors. Chives are perennial and although the top growth dies down each year, it will reappear in spring.

Thyme: *Used in stuffings, soups, and also with fish and duck.*
Sow the seeds between flagstones or in a border in April. Thyme likes a very sunny and dry position where it will grow into a sprawling bush. Like chives, it is perennial and will survive for several years. It is inclined to become straggly as it gets older and a cut back with scissors or shears will do it good.

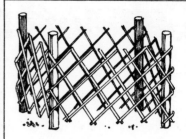

1. Mark out the area with canes and netting.

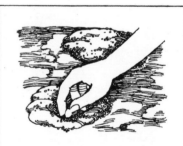

2. Matter is broken down, aided by compost maker.

3. Water in dry weather.

4. Sow marrow seeds on the heap in a pocket of soil.

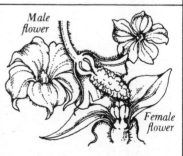

Male flower

Female flower

5. Pollinate female flower.

Compost making

From the chapter on siting the plot in the garden, you will remember that one of the most important ingredients of the soil was humus; the decomposed remains of plants and animals. In growing vegetables you will be throwing away, particularly with root crops, a large amount of plant material – all the leaves and stems. The best way to make use of all this plant material is to plough it back into the soil, enriching it and making it of more use to plants. Gardeners break down the plant material before incorporating it into the soil by using a compost heap. The compost heap need not be a large affair; a metre square is sufficient.

Mark out the area you intend to use with four canes set firmly into the soil. Within these four canes you can deposit any kind of organic waste – if it grows, it will make compost, is a good general rule. Some plastic netting or chicken wire placed over the canes will keep the compost in place.

Put into the heap all the waste from your garden (other than wood, and perennial weeds which have large and permanent root systems) even potato peelings and eggshells from the kitchen. You will be able to buy, from your local garden shop or ironmongers, a packet of 'compost maker' or compost accelerator. This just makes the breakdown process faster and supplies you with compost much sooner than if the material were left to break down on its own. Water the heap in very dry weather.

Sprinkle a layer of the compost maker over the heap every 20 cm. After a year, you will be able to use the compost, from the bottom of the heap first, to dig into your soil – it is particularly useful on the vegetable garden.

As well as using the compost heap as a source of food for the garden, you can also use it as a plot on its own. A marrow or a pumpkin set in soil on the top of a compost heap will provide a tasty crop.

Scrape a hole out of the top of your heap, about 25 cm. across and the same deep, and fill this with ordinary garden soil. Firm the soil well and in late May or early June sow three marrow or pumpkin seeds 2·5 cm deep in the soil. Sow the three in separate places and remove two of them – leaving the strongest – when they have germinated.

Both marrows and pumpkins, being very succulent plants, require lots of water at every stage in their development. Do not overdo this and soak the plant every day, but never allow them to dry out completely. When the stems of the plant are about a metre long, pinch out the tips.

Marrows and pumpkins have male and female flowers on the same plant; the female bears the fruit and pinching out the tips like this will encourage the formation of sideshoots which carry female flowers. You can see the difference between the male and female flowers in the picture. To make sure that the female flower is pollinated and bears fruit, remove a male flower and place the centre of it in the female flower, rubbing off some of the pollen from the male on to the female stigma. This will ensure pollination and all you have to do is to hope that the flower will be fertilized by the pollen and produce a fruit.

Harvest the fruits as soon as they are the size you want – with the pumpkins, allow only four fruits to a plant; two if you want extra large ones. This will probably be in September.

Varieties of marrow: Long White, Long Green.
Varieties of pumpkin: Hundredweight, Hubbard Squash Golden.

Marrow

Enemies...

It would be nice if all the plants in our gardens grew perfectly, but unfortunately this is not the case. From time to time you will notice that either some of the leaves have been eaten or some flowers have been pulled off, or some of the fruit is going rotten. Obviously, it is important to find out what is causing the trouble.

The first thing to realise is that you are not the only living being on your piece of land. It is teeming with animal life of one kind or another; some of them are beneficial to you and your crops, others are not, but they all have a right to be there and you shouldn't interfere with them any more than you have to. If there are only one or two spots on the leaves of your plants, ignore them.

The best remedy for any pest or disease attack is to ensure that the plant is in good soil and is growing well; if it is, then it will have good resistance to minor attacks like this. Unfortunately, not all attacks are minor, even when the plants are growing in good soil. In cases when plants look as though they are about to give up and die, we have to do something about it. The first step is to examine the damage, and the second step is to find out what has caused it. The third step is to stop the plant being damaged any more.

Caterpillars

Slugs: Slugs are one of the worst garden pests. They attack all manner of plants, eating the leaves and sometimes even the stems, especially on seedlings, causing the plants to keel over and die. You can usually spot their slimy trail over the soil around plants which have been damaged. Slugs are particularly active on damp mornings after a warm evening. Individual slugs can be killed by covering them with household salt.

Slug

Greenfly

Greenfly: Greenfly are pests on many plants, especially those which have tender young shoots. The easiest way of killing them in a group is to rub them off the plant with your finger, unpleasant and sticky though it may be. If you have a large attack, mix some washing-up liquid in water to form a nice soapy mixture and spray it on the infected areas of the plant. Repeat this every so often to keep the greenfly down.

Blackfly, which are exactly the same apart from their colour, can be controlled in the same way. On broad beans, however, you can reduce the chances of blackfly attacking your plants by pinching out the growing tip of each plant when two or three flower clusters have been formed. This removes the juiciest part of the plant leaving only the more mature foliage which the flies do not find as tasty.

Wood pigeon

Birds: Many birds are to be encouraged in gardens, indeed it would be a poorer place without them, but certain types of bird can be a tremendous nuisance at times. Sparrows will tear at lettuce leaves, bullfinches will rip the tops off cherry blossom and I have seen a whole row of cauliflowers stripped of their leaves by a pair of pigeons in one afternoon. Keeping birds out of trees is difficult to say the least; without putting a net over the whole tree there is little you can do.

But you can stop them taking the flowers off polyanthuses and crocuses by stringing the plants over with black cotton tied to twigs pushed in the ground. Use ordinary cotton which will snap if they pull at it. I once had to cut some nylon thread off the feet of a blackbird, which hobbled into my garden with the thread cutting into his feet. Tin foil can be cut into strips and hung over seedbeds, but the birds may get used to it and refuse to be scared off.

...and Friends

Caterpillars: When a plant is attacked by caterpillars, the leaves which are eaten will usually still be occupied by the pest. The most effective way to control them is to do a bit of detective work and search for the caterpillars, dropping them into a bucket of hot water when you find them. Cabbages, cauliflowers and nasturtiums are frequently attacked by caterpillars, usually of the cabbage white butterfly or the large white butterfly; it is always a good idea to check in a book so that you know what kind of butterfly the caterpillar is going to turn into. In this way you will avoid killing the larvae of some of our rarer butterflies and moths.

Thrush

Ladybirds

Earthworm

Blackfly

Remember that most of the life in the garden is beneficial. Ladybirds and their larvae eat greenfly and blackfly; birds, particularly starlings and thrushes, eat slugs and snails; worms aerate the soil for us and mix in the humus.

A good general guide to use on insects is that if they are fast moving they usually feed on other insects and are therefore beneficial.

33

Strawberries

On a small plot there is very little room to grow fruit trees but there is usually space in an odd corner to squeeze in two or three strawberry plants grown in a large pot.

If you can obtain a large pot with a diameter at the top of about 25 cm. you will be able to grow three plants in it – just enough to give your family a couple of helpings of delicious fruit in the summer.

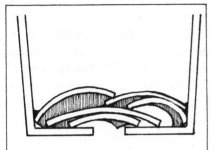

1. Cover drainage holes with broken flower-pot.

Cover the bottom of the pot, over the drainage holes, with a few rough stones or broken pieces of plant pot, laid hollow side down, and fill the pot to the rim with some potting compost which you will be able to buy from your local garden shop. The compost called John Innes Number 3 will be the best one to use. Firm the compost well down.

One-year old plants can be obtained from a nursery in July or August and this is when they should be planted. Space them evenly round the pot, taking care not to plant them too deeply, and water them well.

Strawberries grow best in a sunny spot – a corner on a patio is ideal. Water the plants only when they are dry throughout the winter, but as the weather gets warmer in late March and April they will dry out more frequently and need more regular attention with the watering can. During April and into May, flowers will start to form on the plants and, as the petals fade, the young fruits will begin to develop.

Start feeding the plants once a fortnight with a liquid fertilizer, diluted in the watering can to the manufacturers' directions. As they swell, they will begin to weigh the flower stalks down so that they touch the soil. If this happens the fruits will rot, so place pieces of stick underneath them to keep them off the soil.

To prevent the plants exhausting themselves and to produce larger berries, thin the fruits leaving twelve to fifteen on each plant. As the fruit ripens, it should be picked and eaten fresh; as well as being tasty you will find that the strawberries are also very attractive to look at and their ripening fruits have a tantalizing smell.

2. Grow strawberry plants in potting compost.

3. When young fruit appears use a liquid fertilizer.

4. Keep the fruit clear of the soil with sticks.

5. Thin the fruit out, to twelve or fifteen per plant.

Let's make a rock garden

All over the world, plants are growing in many different kinds of climate. In hot, humid areas are found tropical plants which are tall and lush with bright flowers and succulent fruits. In dry, arid desert areas grow cacti with their water-holding stalks and modified spiny leaves, and under the sea grow seaweeds and other plants which are suited to growing in salt water. These particular habitats would be difficult to reproduce in a British garden, which has a temperate climate and a moderate rainfall and no seashore lapping at its edge.

But we *can* reproduce a habitat which is found in many areas of the world; that of the temperate mountain regions with rocky slopes and particularly well-drained soil. Large amounts of land are not necessary to build a small rock garden where we can accommodate the plants which grow in such a situation.

The most space-saving way of building a rock garden is to construct one in an old sink or bath tub. If you use an old sink – the white porcelain kind – you can mix together some sand, cement and a small quantity of peat which can be turned into a paste by adding water. Painting this on to the outside of the sink will disguise the white shiny surface and will encourage moss to grow over the surface to give the sink a pleasing natural look. By leaving the plug out of the sink you will have a ready-made drainage hole. If you use an old tin bath – not the type installed in houses today, which would be anything but attractive in the garden – make holes in the bottom of it with a garden fork for drainage.

Next place a layer of rubble or broken flower pots in the bottom of your container and fill it up with a mixture of one part garden soil, one part peat, one part sand and one part of washed gravel. This will make a well-drained mixture which will not be too rich for the plants. Firm the soil well in the container and make sure that it is moist.

1. The sink is given a natural look.

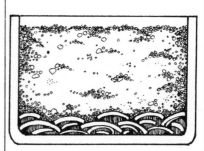

2. Fill sink with a soil, peat, sand and gravel mixture.

35

3. Arrange the rocks in an attractive pattern.

4. Sink the rocks into the soil and make them firm.

5. Plant alpines in late summer or early autumn.

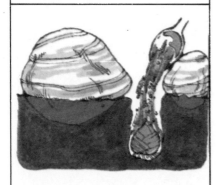

6. Dwarf bulbs can be planted in September or October.

Now you have to do the landscape work. Search around either in the garden or in a place where you know there are a few rocks or even large stones which you can use, and select two or three pieces you think would look best in your container. Don't pick too many or there will not be enough room for the plants. When you have picked your pieces of stone, try positioning them on top of the soil, moving them around until you find a pattern which is attractive.

Remember that when you see rocks in their natural surroundings, the layers in the rock, known as strata, are usually to be found running the same way. Arrange yours so that they do the same. Sink at least a third of the rock into the soil to hold it firm and to make it appear as though much more of the rock is buried beneath the surface.

Now we come to the planting. Most alpine plants, which is the name given to plants which grow on any mountain, not just the alps, flower in the spring and early summer, so they are best planted in late summer or early autumn. Dwarf bulbs which are at their best during the winter months make a useful extension of the flowering period and can be planted in September or October between the other plants.

The plants shown here will make a good display in a sink garden and provide a long flowering season.

Alpines: thyme, phlox, aubrieta, rock rose, houseleek, pinks, saxifrage.

Bulbs: dwarf irises, dwarf narcissus, snowdrops, crocuses.

Planting a dwarf conifer in the sink will give it more height and will add to the miniature effect of the garden which will appear like a large piece of land looked at through the wrong end of a telescope; this will complete an attractive little rock garden.

Phlox

Rock rose

Pink

Thyme

Aubrieta

Houseleek

Saxifrage

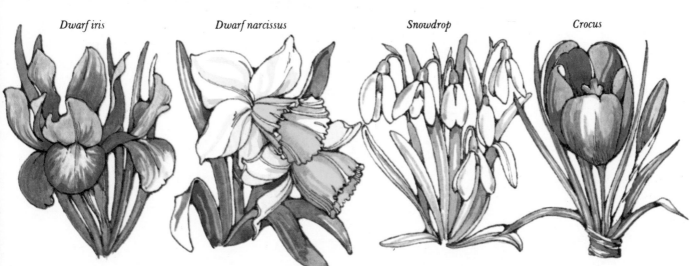

Dwarf iris   *Dwarf narcissus*   *Snowdrop*   *Crocus*

A garden pool

Constructing a small pool will not only give you a chance to grow a wider range of plants, but it will also enable you to bring other forms of wild life to your garden. Apart from fish, which you can introduce yourself, different kinds of wild birds will visit your garden for the benefit of the water and you may even find a nomadic frog taking up residence.

Like any form of garden, the water garden can be as big or as small as you want it to be. It can be made out of half an oil drum or you can make a pool any shape you wish by using a polythene or P.V.C. pool liner. Before you start to construct your pool, think of the best place in the garden to site it. It is no use placing it near trees, where it will be shaded in the summer and full of leaves in the winter; pick an open but sheltered site so that the pool gets plenty of sun but is sheltered from strong winds.

Now is the time to decide what kind of pool you want to make. If you want to use a ready-made container, the hole you will have to take out will be governed by the size of the vessel. Apart from half an oil drum you could use an old bread crock, a barrel or even an old sink or tin bath.

When you fill in the hole around the container, be sure that the container is level and that the soil is packed evenly to prevent rocking. There is no reason why you should not have the container free-standing if you do not want to bury it – a small water tub of plants will provide a pleasing display on a patio.

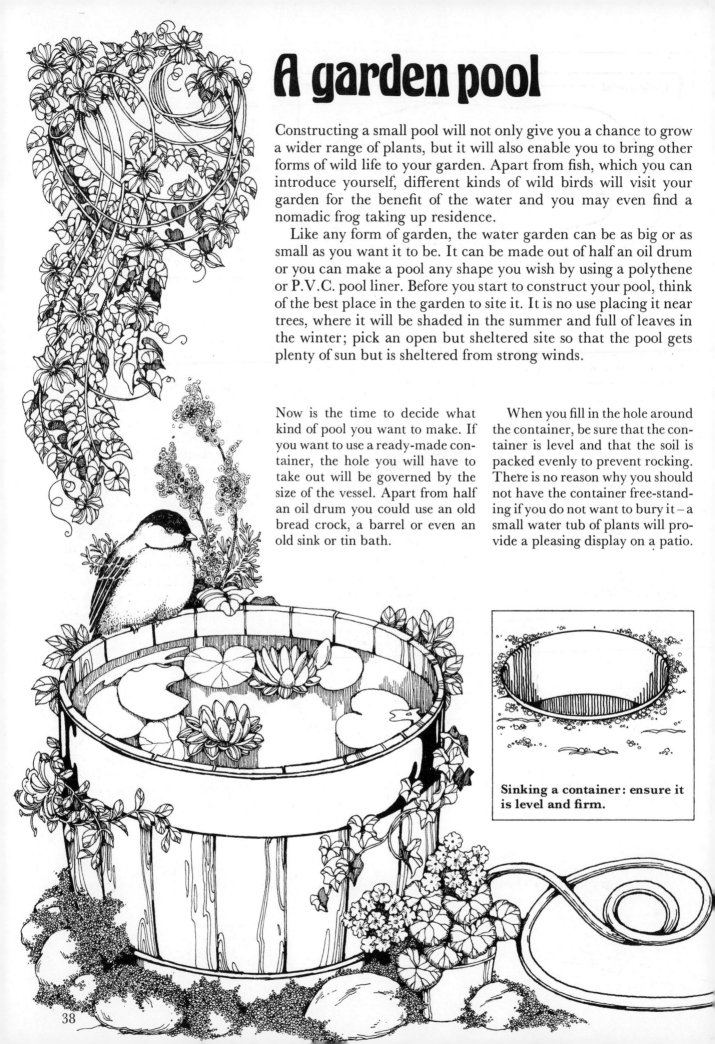

Sinking a container: ensure it is level and firm.

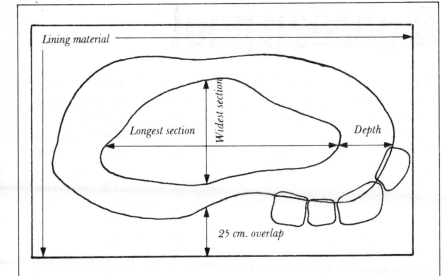

1. Draw a scale diagram of the pool; allow enough material for the depth of the pool, and allow for an overlap at the side.

2. Dig hole, heaping soil at one end. Remove sharp stones.

4. Weight down overlap with broken flagstones (or turf).

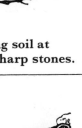

3. Smooth down lining. Take care not to make holes.

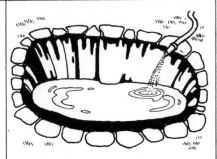

5. Fill pool slowly with hose pipe.

If you want to be a bit more adventurous and make a pool to your own design, sketch out the sort of shape you want on a piece of paper before going out to sculpt the soil. Draw the diagram to scale so that you can work out how much of the lining material you will need, remembering to allow for the depth of the pool as well.

Don't make the pool too deep – a depth of 30 to 45 cm. is ample. The cheapest liner will be black polythene but this will only last a year or two and the extra amount of money spent on P.V.C. will soon be justified as this is much longer lasting. You will be able to buy both materials by the metre and they will probably be 90 cm. or 122 cm. wide. Before starting to dig out the hole, decide where you are going to put the soil – it might be useful for constructing a bank.

Having dug your hole to the correct shape, take any rough or sharp stones out of the sides and carefully lower the liner into it. Smooth out the material taking great care not to make any holes in it (they are very difficult to find afterwards) and spread it over the whole surface of the pool shape, tucking it in to fit the sides.

When this is done, the sides will need weighting down; broken flagstones are ideal and they can be used to make a permanent edging. Failing this, you could take grass turfs right up to the side.

Now is the time to introduce the water. Filling the pool with buckets would take you days; use a hose pipe and allow it to trickle in fairly slowly so that the water gradually weighs down the liner and pushes it against the sides of the pool. Fill to within 10 cm. of the rim.

The best time for planting up the pool is spring – the plants will grow straight away and not suffer much of a check. If you allow the water to flow over the edge of the polythene at one side, you will create an area which will be just the environment needed by bog plants. Here you can grow the moisture-loving irises, astilbes (which used to be called spiraeas), primulas with their many-coloured flowers – some nodding and some in a tiered candelabra arrangement; hostas – the plantain lilies – and also the marsh marigold or kingcup.

Primula

Hosta

Waterlilies

Duckweed

Iris

Marsh marigold

In the pool, planted in plastic baskets which you can buy from a nursery, you can place the plants which prefer their roots actually in the water.

The best known of these is the water lily which gives a marvellous show of flowers and leaves right through the summer. Water lilies should be planted in spring in heavy soil which will not float away when the basket is sub-

merged. Trim off the long, thick anchorage roots on the lily, and plant it in the basket at the level it was planted previously. Never let the plant dry out. When the lily has been planted, cover the surface of the soil in the basket with gravel, having rammed the soil quite firmly into place. This will ensure that as little of the soil as possible will be dislodged. Sink the plant into the water slowly, standing the

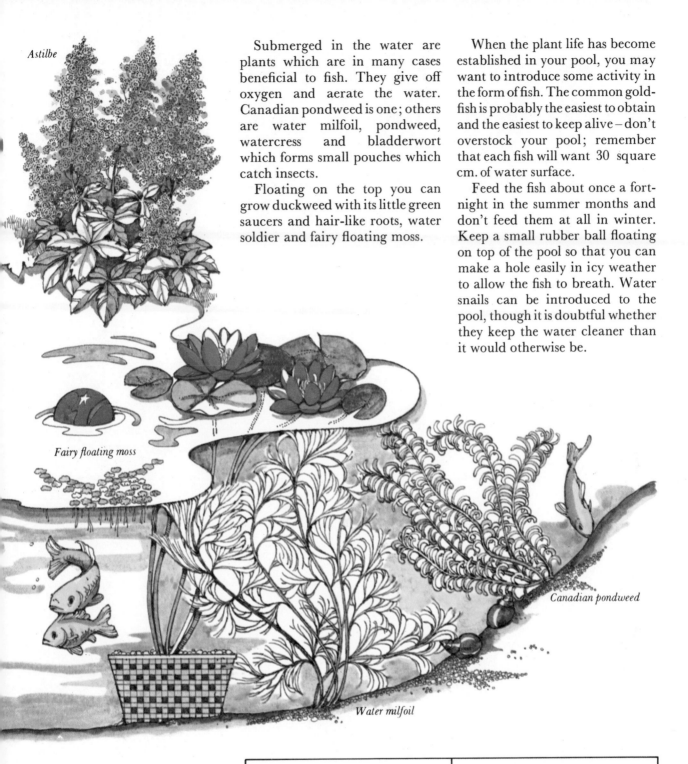

Astilbe

Fairy floating moss

Canadian pondweed

Water milfoil

Submerged in the water are plants which are in many cases beneficial to fish. They give off oxygen and aerate the water. Canadian pondweed is one; others are water milfoil, pondweed, watercress and bladderwort which forms small pouches which catch insects.

Floating on the top you can grow duckweed with its little green saucers and hair-like roots, water soldier and fairy floating moss.

When the plant life has become established in your pool, you may want to introduce some activity in the form of fish. The common gold-fish is probably the easiest to obtain and the easiest to keep alive – don't overstock your pool; remember that each fish will want 30 square cm. of water surface.

Feed the fish about once a fort-night in the summer months and don't feed them at all in winter. Keep a small rubber ball floating on top of the pool so that you can make a hole easily in icy weather to allow the fish to breath. Water snails can be introduced to the pool, though it is doubtful whether they keep the water cleaner than it would otherwise be.

basket on bricks at first so that the leaves rest on top of the water. As the leaf stalks extend, you can gradually lower the lily to the bottom of the pool until the basket sits on the bottom. Suitable varieties of water lily for small pools include *Nymphaea odorata*, a white, scented variety, and *Nymphaea froebeli* which is red. Both of these are available from most nurseries which sell aquatic plants.

1. Water lily: trim off long anchorage roots.

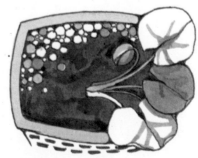

2. Plant in basket. Cover packed soil with gravel.

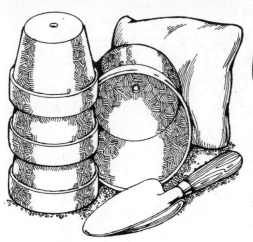

A garden frame

By equipping your garden with a small and easily made frame, you will find that you are able to sow vegetables and flowers several weeks earlier than is possible outside, and you will be able to take food and flowers to the table sooner than before. There is no need to heat the frame, it will be sufficiently warm with just a sheet of glass or a piece of polythene over the top.

Making the Frame

A frame is easily constructed from either a wooden box or bits of old floorboard or flat timber. The one in the diagram measures 60 cm. × 1 m. and is quite large enough to take pots of seeds in spring, a cucumber in the summer and some lettuce in the autumn.

If you build a frame this size, use two sheets of glass as a cover rather than one as they will be easier to lift off and replace. If you use polythene, stretch it to a light wooden frame and hold it in place with tacks. Remove all weeds from the ground inside the frame and rake the soil level.

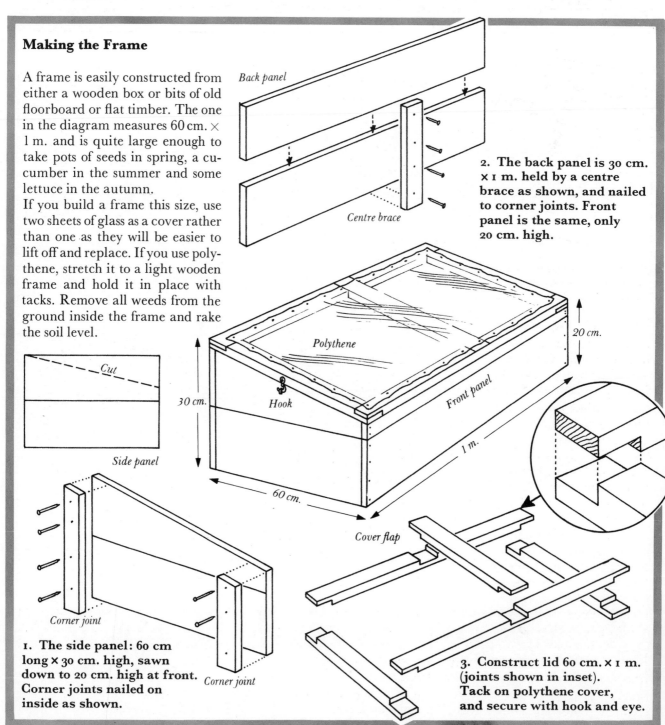

Back panel

Centre brace

2. The back panel is 30 cm. × 1 m. held by a centre brace as shown, and nailed to corner joints. Front panel is the same, only 20 cm. high.

Polythene

20 cm.

Hook

Front panel

30 cm.

Cut

Side panel

1 m.

60 cm.

Cover flap

Corner joint

Corner joint

1. The side panel: 60 cm long × 30 cm. high, sawn down to 20 cm. high at front. Corner joints nailed on inside as shown.

3. Construct lid 60 cm. × 1 m. (joints shown in inset). Tack on polythene cover, and secure with hook and eye.

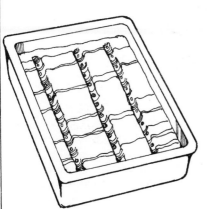

1. February: sow cauliflower 1.25 cm. deep in seedbox.

2. Water seedbox and place in frame.

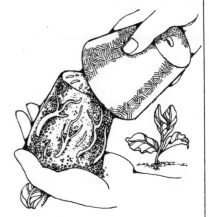

4. When 10 cm. high plant out about 40 cm. apart.

In about February, sow some cauliflower seed in a shallow seedbox. Use John Innes Seed Compost which you can get from a nursery or shop. (The John Innes Composts are a range of soil mixtures which contain soil, peat and sand and a certain amount of fertilizer. There is one Seed Compost and three Potting Composts numbered from one to three. Number three has three times as much fertilizer as Number one and is therefore used on larger plants requiring more nutrients.) Sow the seeds 1·25 cm. deep. Water the box well and place it in the frame, covering it with the glass or polythene. When the seedlings are about 5 cm. high, they can be planted in small pots using John Innes Number 1 Potting Compost, which contains more nutrition than the seed compost. Check the seedlings daily and water them whenever they are dry.

3. When 5 cm. high transfer to pots of potting compost.

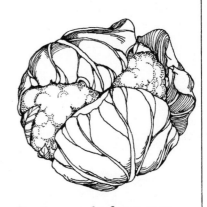

5. Bend over a leaf or two to protect white centre.

Ventilate the frame by lifting the glass on warm days for the first four weeks, and eventually leave the glass off each day, replacing it at night. This is known as hardening off. When the plants are about 10 cm. high, they can be planted out on your plot about 40 cm. apart and firmed well.

Water them in to give them a good start. As the white centres, which are called curds, begin to develop, bend in one or two of the leaves to protect them from the weather and keep them white. When the separate sections of the curd are distinguishable, the cauliflower can be cut. Good varieties to use are Conquest and White Heart.

Apart from vegetables, you can also raise half-hardy annual flower seeds in the frame. These are more tender than hardy annuals and will not stand the lower temperatures in spring. If you sow them in your frame though, you will be able to plant them out shortly after your hardy annuals have germinated, and they will flower at the same time. Here are some suitable ones to use: French marigolds, antirrhinums, Coltness dahlias, salvias, asters, and nemesia.

Sow each of the different types of seed in a separate pot of John Innes Seed Compost. Water them and label each pot clearly, showing the variety, and date of sowing.

Ventilate the frame on warm days. When the seeds germinate, you can transplant them into a seedbox containing John Innes Number 1 Compost, again using one box for each kind and labelling them. Insert them with a small dibber, making sure that they are firmed in. Water the seedlings as they need it and ventilate the frame well.

When the weather gets warmer, the glass can be removed altogether during the day and replaced at night. In late May, the plants can be planted out.

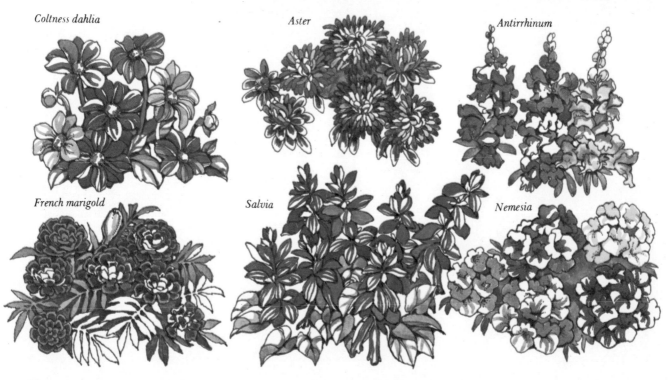

Coltness dahlia

Aster

Antirrhinum

French marigold

Salvia

Nemesia

During the summer months you may like to grow a cucumber in the frame. Sow two seeds in an 8 cm. pot in April and germinate them in the house, covering the pot with a small piece of glass and a sheet of paper. When the seedlings germinate, remove the glass and paper and pull out the weakest of the seedlings when they are about 5 cm. high.

Harden off the remaining seedling in the garden frame by ventilating it a little more each day. In late May, when the glass is being left off all day and replaced at night, enrich the soil in the frame with some well-rotted manure and draw the soil up to form a mound.

Plant the young cucumber firmly in the top of the mound and water it well in. Pinch out the growing tip when the plant has made six leaves and allow four side shoots to develop. Stop each of these when they have made two leaves; this encourages fruiting.

Pin these four shoots to the soil in the frame using thin wire – space them out evenly. When male flowers are formed they should be removed at once. The fruit will swell without fertilization and if the flowers are fertilized the fruits will taste bitter. The picture shows the difference between the male and female flowers.

Water the plant with diluted liquid fertilizer as the fruits begin to swell and when they develop place a piece of wood or glass underneath them to prevent rotting. Pick the fruits when they are large enough. Good varieties are Improved Telegraph and Butcher's Disease Resisting.

To grow autumn lettuces in your frame, remove the cucumber plant in late August and level out the soil. Sow a lettuce variety such as Imperial Winter or Arctic King as described in the chapter dealing with vegetables, but give them the protection of your frame, ventilating well during the day and closing it down at night. You will be able to harvest the lettuces in spring.

1. **April: sow two cucumber seeds in a pot.**

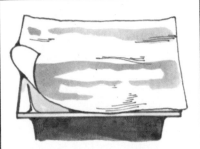

2. **Cover with glass and paper: germinate indoors.**

3. **Choose strongest seedling and harden off in frame.**

5. **Pinch out for fruiting.**

Male flower

Female flower

7. **Remove male flowers.**

4. **Plant in frame in mound of manured soil.**

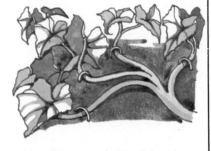

6. **Pin shoots to soil with wire.**

8. **Stop fruit rotting on soil.**

Troughs for the terrace

By planting up a container which is large enough to hold a number of plants, but small enough to be reasonably portable, you can produce an attractive plant grouping which can be moved around the garden or patio to provide a splash of colour wherever it is needed. By replanting the container when one group of plants has finished flowering, it is possible to obtain almost year-round flower effect.

A wide variety of tubs and troughs are now available in the shops but it is much more fun to make your own from bits and pieces you can find in the garden shed or the garage.

Making the Trough

The easiest way to make a trough is to knock one together from spare pieces of wood – the shape of the container depending on the size and shape of the pieces of wood that are available. The trough can be painted to suit any colour scheme. The diagram shows the sort of trough you could construct.

1. **The size is up to you. 1 m. × 20 cm. × 20 cm. should be adequate. Drill drainage holes about 4 cm. apart in base before nailing on side panels.**

2. **Attach front and back panels as shown.**

3. **Nail two blocks to the base to raise off ground.**

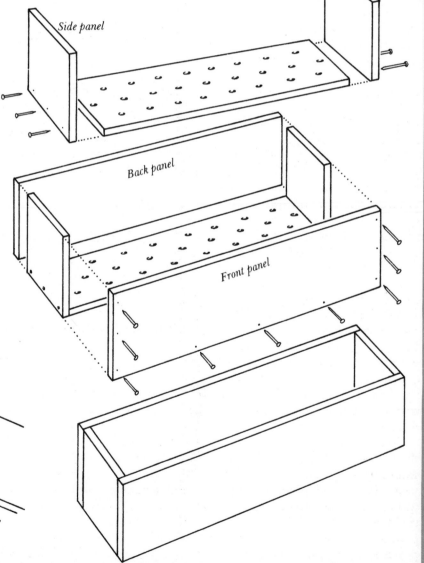

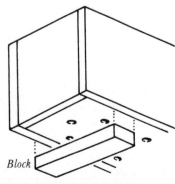

3. The plants should go in first . . .

4. . . . followed by the bulbs, planted in between.

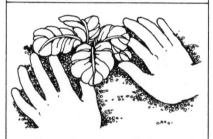

5. Firm the soil well down among the plants.

6. Water the plants in. Place trough in a sunny spot.

If you can find a log and persuade someone to remove most of the centre of it you can drill some holes in the base to produce a container with a natural rustic appearance.

It is very important that whatever form of trough or tub you use, it has plenty of drainage holes which should be covered with a good layer of stones or broken flower pots. If good drainage is not ensured, the soil will quickly become waterlogged and the plants will die as a result. It is also important to use a good compost in the trough. As the plants' roots are in a confined space, they will need all the nutrition they can get and this should be supplied by filling the tub or trough with a compost like John Innes Potting Compost Number 2 which contains plenty of plant foods. During the growing season the plants will also benefit from a fortnightly application of a diluted liquid fertilizer.

To provide flower colour almost the whole year round, the trough will have to be planted up twice a year, first in September using spring-flowering plants, and then in May using summer-flowering plants. The following plants will provide a good display of colour at the times shown.

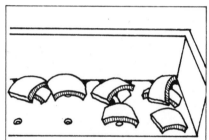

1. Cover drainage holes with stones or broken pot.

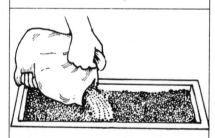

2. Fill trough with potting compost.

For a spring display: Plant mixed colours of polyanthuses, forget-me-nots and pansies and underplant them with bulbs such as grape hyacinths, daffodils, tulips and hyacinths. Keep the display to one or two colours if you wish by planting only matching or complementary shades of flowers.

Using a trowel, insert the plants first and plant the bulbs around them; this avoids disturbing the bulbs when they have been planted and stops them growing through the centre of the plants. Firm the soil well around the plants and water them in. The trough should be stood in a spot which is sunny but sheltered from strong winds. It will need only occasional watering until the plants start to grow, when larger supplies may be needed; feeding is not really necessary on the spring-flowering display as it is the first planting in the trough.

1. Work general fertilizer into the soil.

2. Fuchsias can now be planted successfully.

3. Annuals are ideal for the trough in summer.

4. Water with liquid fertilizer every two weeks.

For a summer display: Remove the bulbs and plants from the trough in April or May when they have finished flowering. The bulbs can be planted in the garden, as can the polyanthuses, forget-me-nots and pansies, which you could place in an out-of-the-way spot for lifting and planting in the trough again the following year. The spring display will have taken much nourishment out of the soil, so a couple of handfuls of general fertilizer worked into the compost will be beneficial. Stir the compost up well with a trowel and then firm it back into place. You may find that you have to top up the trough with compost each time you remove plants.

The summer display can now be planted. Annuals are excellent plants to use in troughs; they grow rapidly and flower quite soon after planting. Some of the best are trailing lobelia, french marigolds, alyssum, petunias and salvias. Along with these you can plant geraniums, fuchsias or even a dwarf conifer. The annuals can be raised in the garden frame and planted into your trough when it is ready. You will probably need only one or two geraniums or fuchsias and these you could buy from a garden shop, keeping them in pots indoors over the winter to use again the following year.

Water the trough well during the summer and remember to feed it every two weeks. There should not be many weeds appearing in the trough; those which do can be pulled out when they are quite small so that they do not smother the other plants.

Bottle gardens

Gardens constructed in bottles are attractive for many reasons; they create a miniature environment which, if imaginatively designed, will provide hours of fascination. They are reasonably cheap to construct and, perhaps most important of all, they are very easy to maintain, requiring little or no attention once they are planted. Gardens can be constructed in a variety of bottles, from the large acid bottles called carboys, to sweet jars, large pickle jars and cider flagons.

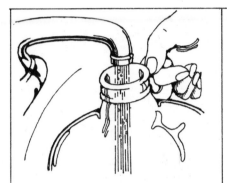

1. **Choose a bottle and wash it out thoroughly.**

3. **Firm the soil well with a cotton reel on a stick.**

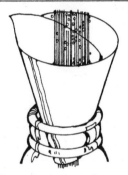

2. **Pour in 8 cm. of compost through a funnel.**

4. **Larger-necked bottles can be filled by hand.**

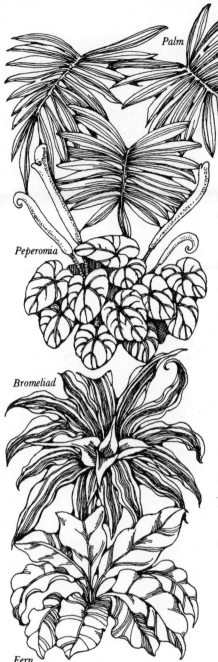

Palm

Peperomia

Bromeliad

Fern

Once you have obtained a suitable container, wash it out thoroughly to clear it of any remains of the previous contents. The best compost to use for bottle gardens is John Innes Seed Compost, an 8 cm. layer being sufficient in most cases. If you have a large bottle you can contour the soil making it deeper at one side and creating a miniature hill. With carboys and other narrow-necked bottles, filling with soil and planting are made more difficult; larger-necked bottles are considerably easier.

To insert the compost, take a piece of paper and form a cone-shaped funnel; the soil can be fed into the neck through this, but take care to stop it touching the sides where it will stick. Firm the soil well with a cotton reel stuck on to the end of a cane – this tool is also useful when planting up the bottle. Larger-necked bottles can be filled and planted by hand; the sweet jars being either stood up or laid on their sides.

Plants for bottle gardens should be chosen very carefully. Avoid rampant plants like tradescantia which will quickly swamp slower growing specimens and fill the container. The plants you use will be those which like a humid environment and are reasonably compact in habit. Those I have found suitable are the aluminium plant (pilea), peperomias, small palms, bromeliads, ferns, slow-growing ivies and crotons. In all cases pick plants which will have room to grow in your bottle and avoid using too many. Leave them room to grow.

Aluminium plant

Croton

Ivy

Making the Tools

With most narrow-necked bottles you will have to design a series of planting tools which can be operated through the neck of the bottle. I have mentioned one already; the cotton reel on the end of a cane which is used for firming. Others you can make are: a teaspoon fastened to the end of a cane, to make holes for the plants and also to fill in around the plant when it is inserted; a long wire hook for positioning the plants when you have dropped them into the bottle. By using these as shown in the diagram, you should be able to plant up your container without too much trouble.

Right: a selection of the tools you may care to make. Bind each item to a long, thin piece of cane.

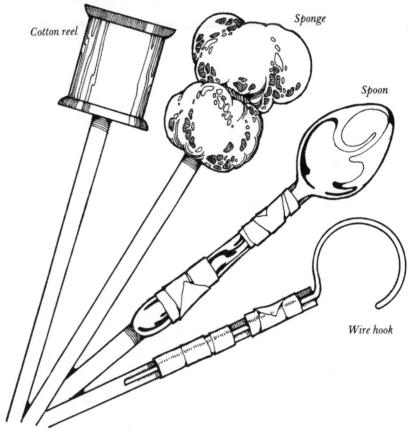

Cotton reel

Sponge

Spoon

Wire hook

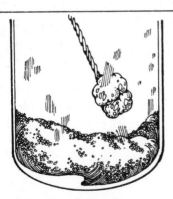

1. Use the sponge for condensation on the inside of the glass.

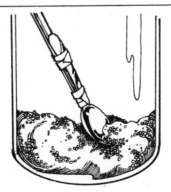

2. The spoon is used as a miniature trowel.

3. The hook is used to position the plant in the bottle.

Make a hole for the plant with the spoon, knock it out of its pot and squeeze the root ball so that it will drop through the neck of the bottle. Ease the plant into the hole and firm it with the cotton reel. When all the plants are firmly in place, water the soil using a watering can with a long spout. Run the water down the inside of the bottle to avoid displacing the soil. When this is done, seal the bottle with its cap and the job is finished.

1. **Make a hole in the soil: ease roots through neck.**

2. **Firm soil round the plant with cotton reel.**

3. **Water down the inside through long spout.**

The garden will need no further attention. Avoid placing the bottle garden in full sun where the plants will lose water rapidly and cause condensation to develop on the sides of the bottle, but do not place it in a dark corner. The bottle may steam up for a short time after planting but this will soon subside leaving only a slight film of water which in no way stops the plants being seen.

When the garden becomes overgrown, remove the plants and soil and reconstruct using new seed compost and the same plants thinned out; unless, of course, you wish to introduce some new ones and start a new bottle garden.

Miniature gardens indoors

It is possible to construct miniature gardens in a wide variety of containers. Apart from the usual pots and bowls, gardens can be made in large brandy glasses, goldfish bowls, fish tanks, wine bottles and even old gramophone records.

To make a garden in a goldfish bowl, brandy glass or fish tank, follow the same procedure as you would for a bottle garden, using the same compost and plants. The main difference with these gardens is that they are open to the air and will need watering as they dry out. Be particularly careful about this; there are no drainage holes in the bottom of the containers and it will be easy to overwater. Do not water the plants until the soil around them is dry to the touch.

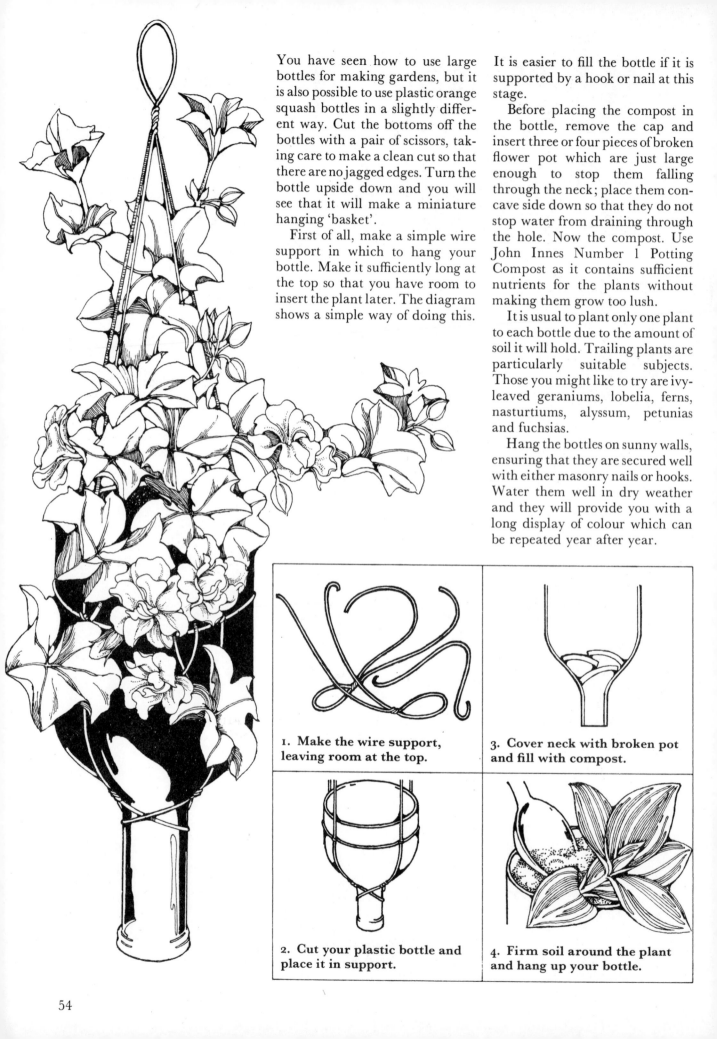

You have seen how to use large bottles for making gardens, but it is also possible to use plastic orange squash bottles in a slightly different way. Cut the bottoms off the bottles with a pair of scissors, taking care to make a clean cut so that there are no jagged edges. Turn the bottle upside down and you will see that it will make a miniature hanging 'basket'.

First of all, make a simple wire support in which to hang your bottle. Make it sufficiently long at the top so that you have room to insert the plant later. The diagram shows a simple way of doing this.

It is easier to fill the bottle if it is supported by a hook or nail at this stage.

Before placing the compost in the bottle, remove the cap and insert three or four pieces of broken flower pot which are just large enough to stop them falling through the neck; place them concave side down so that they do not stop water from draining through the hole. Now the compost. Use John Innes Number 1 Potting Compost as it contains sufficient nutrients for the plants without making them grow too lush.

It is usual to plant only one plant to each bottle due to the amount of soil it will hold. Trailing plants are particularly suitable subjects. Those you might like to try are ivy-leaved geraniums, lobelia, ferns, nasturtiums, alyssum, petunias and fuchsias.

Hang the bottles on sunny walls, ensuring that they are secured well with either masonry nails or hooks. Water them well in dry weather and they will provide you with a long display of colour which can be repeated year after year.

1. Make the wire support, leaving room at the top.

3. Cover neck with broken pot and fill with compost.

2. Cut your plastic bottle and place it in support.

4. Firm soil around the plant and hang up your bottle.

Old 78 r.p.m. gramophone records can also be made into containers for miniature gardens— when they are unsuitable for playing. Immerse the record in hot water and you will find that it will become pliable and easy to bend. Bend it into a suitable shape with your hands, take it out and allow it to cool again and it will become rigid in its new shape. You now have a container which even possesses a drainage hole in the base.

The record can now be used to make a miniature garden. Plant it up with stones, moss, seedling trees and miniature plants from hedgerows and the garden and it will last for several weeks. Each plant can be removed when it has finished flowering and replaced by another one yet to bloom. You can even include a pool in your garden by sinking in a small container of water, and keeping it filled up. Your garden is now complete.

1. Place an old 78 r.p.m. record in hot water. Wear rubber gloves!

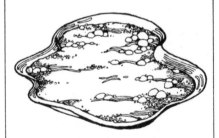

3. After crocking, fill with potting compost, and make a landscape.

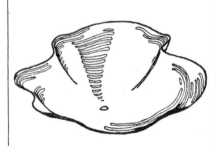

2. Bend record into an attractive shape, and let it cool.

4. Add plants and moss to make a miniature garden.

House plants

No house is really complete without a selection of plants on its tables and windowsills. In return for a small amount of care and attention they will provide interest and colour the whole year round.

Many house plants are killed by kindness. Some owners are apt to think that they need to be watered every day and in these circumstances it is seldom very long before the plants curl up and die. A few plants need to be wet all the time, but the vast majority need only be watered when the soil is dry to the touch and as a general rule this is the key to success. Plants should not be watered on a regular basis – it is obvious that on a warm, sunny day the soil will dry out more rapidly than on a dull, cloudy day and more water will be needed in such conditions. In winter plants will need watering much less frequently.

It is a good idea to start by growing some of the easier house plants and to move on to the more difficult ones when you have mastered these. Some easily grown house plants are: busy lizzie, kangaroo vine, coleus, tradescantia, spider plant, variegated ivy and the different coloured geraniums.

1. Cut off a 10 cm. shoot.

2. Remove lower leaves.

3. Stand in water until roots sprout.

4. Pot in No. 1 compost.

Many plants can be started from cuttings. Busy lizzie and tradescantia are very easy to propagate in this way. From a mature plant, remove a shoot about 10 cm. long. Using a sharp knife, trim it cleanly below a leaf joint. Remove the leaves from the bottom 5 cm. of the stem and stand the cutting in a glass of water on a windowsill. After a few weeks you will see roots emerging from the stem base and the young plant can be potted into an 8 cm. pot of John Innes Number 1 Potting Compost. Take great care not to damage the roots at this stage. Water the plant in and grow it on a windowsill for the next week or so until the roots are established.

Apart from watering, house plants should be kept free of dust (a feather duster is ideal for this purpose) and their tips should be pinched out when they become tall and leggy; this will encourage the plant to branch and become bushy. Feed the plants every two weeks during the summer, using a diluted liquid fertilizer. In winter, feeding is not necessary and watering can be carried out only occasionally, when really dry.

1. Repotting: be careful not to damage the roots.

2. Repot in a larger pot of No. 2 compost.

When a plant has been in one pot for over a year, it is advisable to replant it into a larger pot – the roots will have exhausted the food in the smaller one. Insert the plant in a pot 4 or 5 cm. larger than the last one and use John Innes Number 2 Potting Compost which contains a larger supply of plant nutrients than the Number 1 Compost.

When you have mastered the more simple subjects you might like to try growing plants like gloxinias, African violets, rubber plants and maidenhair ferns which need a little more skill. In most cases, watering is the key to success – if you master this, there is no end to what you can grow.

A garden on your windowsill

Gardening is a hobby which can occupy as much space as you have available, but it can also be practised in a very limited area. An indoor windowsill may be all the room you can spare for plants, particularly if you live in a flat and have no garden.

Apart from house plants, bulbs in bowls, mustard and cress and miniature gardens, the windowsill gardener can grow a wide variety of plants for amusement. Various kinds of pips are fascinating to watch as they develop; date stones, orange pips, apple pips and avocado pear stones can be sown, and so long as you do not expect fruits the following year you will enjoy watching the development of the plants at every stage in their growth. It is quite possible to pick fruit from orange trees grown from pips, but this will take at least five or six years in most cases and because of cross-pollination, the plants may not produce fruit as good as that from which the pip was taken.

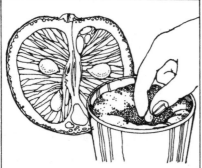

1. Plant orange pips in pot of compost; keep in a dark warm cupboard until germination.

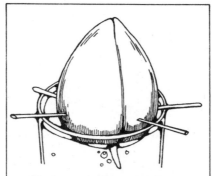

3. Soak avocado stone for a day. Place over jar, held by cocktail sticks.

2. Put in a sunny place. Repot to individual pots when the plants are 5 cm. high.

4. When shoot and roots grow plant avocado in compost, and repot as it grows.

Bulb growing can be given an added attraction if the bulbs are grown in water rather than fibre. By using this method of cultivation you will be able to watch the roots growing. Coffee jars, pickle jars and long tumblers can all be used. The bulb is simply placed on the top with its base just touching the water. As the roots begin to grow, they will extend into the water, filling the container with a white network of activity. The bulbs will flower at the same time as those grown in fibre and the only attention they need is an occasional topping up with water.

Hyacinths are perhaps the best bulbs to grow in this fashion, the only problem being that they are sometimes inclined to topple over. A piece of wire about 20 cm. long will prevent this happening if it is pushed through the bulb and down to the bottom of the container, where it will act as a balance. The roots will make a fascinating display.

1. **Place bulb over the jar, let roots grow into the water.**

3. **Peanuts: remove shells and plant three nuts in compost.**

4. **The plant forces the nuts into the soil.**

2. **Wire can be pushed through the bulb to act as a balance.**

Peanuts are great fun to grow. They produce only two or three nuts on a plant but are an amusing novelty. Remove the outer casings and sow three nuts in an 8 cm. pot of John Innes Number 1 Potting Compost. Sow the seeds in April and germinate them on a warm windowsill, taking care that the soil does not dry out. When the plants are about 10 cm. tall, repot them singly into 12 cm. pots and grow them on.

When the flowers begin to fade, you will see the stalks bend downwards and force the fruits into the soil where they will mature. Water the plants slightly less at this point so that the nuts do not rot. At the end of the year you can knock the plants out of their pots and eat the nuts, though you will only harvest three or four from each plant at the most!

A diary

It is both interesting and useful to keep a diary of what you do in the garden – particularly if things go wrong and you want to see how to avoid making the same mistakes next year. Use it to record the date when you sowed a particular plant, when it germinated, when you thinned out the seedlings and when it flowered or fruited. By doing this you will know when to sow next year if you want to pick flowers or vegetables at a particular time. If your peas matured later than you would have liked, you can sow them earlier next year; if your half-hardy annuals were nipped by frost you can plant out later next year. Make sure you record everything of interest – you will forget about the things you try to keep in your head.

You can divide your diary into sections for each type of plant you grow, making it easier to see what you did to a particular group of plants. The diagram gives some idea of the sort of layout you could adopt.

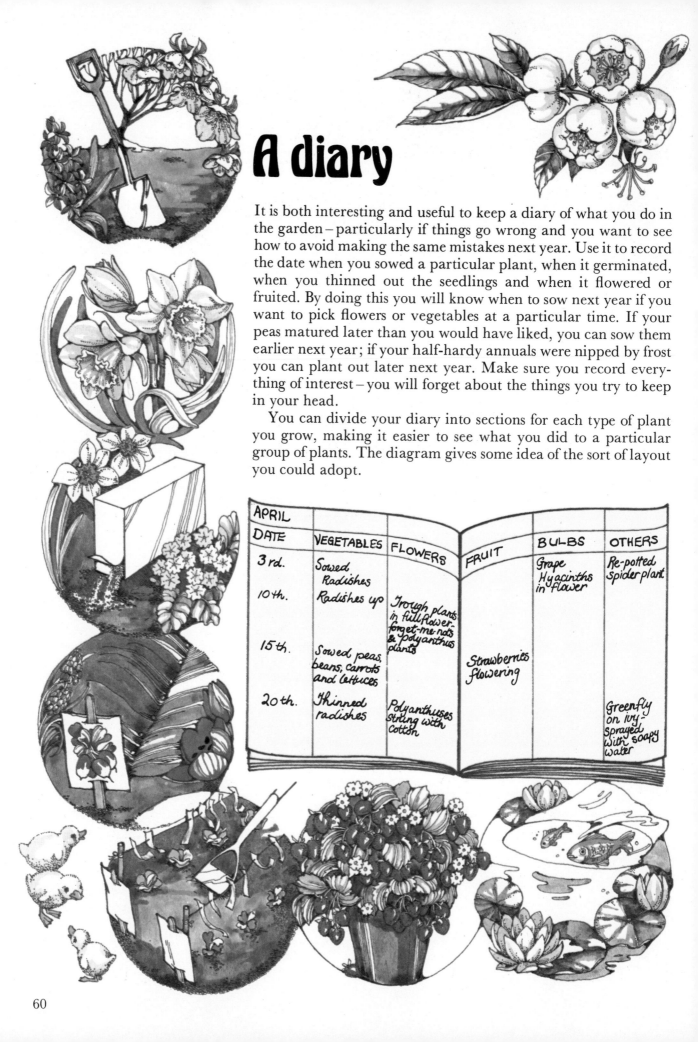

APRIL DATE	VEGETABLES	FLOWERS	FRUIT	BULBS	OTHERS
3rd.	Sowed Radishes			Grape Hyacinths in flower	Re-potted Spider plant
10th.	Radishes up	Trough plants in full flower – forget-me-nots & polyanthus plants			
15th.	Sowed peas, beans, carrots and lettuces		Strawberries flowering		
20th.	Thinned radishes	Polyanthuses strung with cotton			Greenfly on ivy – sprayed with soapy water

There is no beginning or end to the gardener's year. Sowing and growing goes on the year round and, as you soon find when you have done some gardening, flowers can be enjoyed at any time of the year and a remarkable range of fruits and vegetables can be produced in their seasons.

Don't think, either, that because your garden is small there is little scope to do exciting things. Even if you have only a window-sill, pot plants can be grown for their flowers. A back yard or a paved area can be just the place for plants in pots.

Certainly gardening calls for patience and determination but the chances are that, like me, you will find it the most rewarding of hobbies.